TRUE AND TACKY II

MORE WEIRD STORIES
from the World's Newswires

Carolyn Naifeh & Monica Hoose

Illustrations by Bob Staake

TOPPER BOOKS

AN IMPRINT OF PHAROS BOOKS • A SCRIPPS HOWARD COMPANY
NEW YORK

Contents

Games People Play 1

Battle of the Sexes 17

New and Improved 32

Tell 'em Charlie Sent Ya 39

I've Fallen and I Can't Get Up 42

Beam Me Up 49

Hair Today, Gone Tomorrow 55

Prickly Problems 63

We Are Family 71

A Race to the Finish 78

Ain't You Got No Culture? 87

Mad Menagerie 100

I Couldn't Help Myself 113

Car 54, Where Are You? 118

Acknowledgments

Our gratitude to Mel Berger and Shari Jee. And a special thanks to Preston Amos, Tim Andrews, Erin Brummett, Martha Clarke, Bob Dore, Ralph Eckhardt, John Farris, Norm Goldstein, Al Green, Ravi M. Khanna, Neils Lindquist, George Meek, Annette Miller, Jacques Thomet, Jim Trengrove, and Brian Williams.

Games People Play

What's in a Name?
In 'Jamie's' Case,
It's 1,023 Letters

HOUSTON (AP) — CoSandra Williams says she spent years planning her daughter's name. It may take that long before the girl can say it.

The six-year-old girl has more than 1,000 letters in her first name—and has earned a spot in the *Guinness Book of Records*.

The name is so long the girl has two nicknames: Jameshauwnnel or Jamie to most of her friends.

"I wanted to get away from those old, plain names we've been using for so many years," said Mrs. Williams, twenty-nine, who started making up the name in the tenth grade.

The name, a compilation of more than 100 shorter first names, has 1,023 letters and two apostrophes. The girl's middle name is relatively short, just thirty-six letters.

The first name includes monikers of many of the girl's relatives, the names of several countries and cities, and terms such as *friend* and *love*. It also includes two kinds of cars, including the Corvette, which Mrs. Williams chose to spell *corvett*, and the titles of a couple of movies, including *Cleopatra*, which she spelled *cleonpatra*.

Jameshauwnnel can't write her given name, or even say most of it, but she says she likes it.

Mrs. Williams told her former husband that he could name any male children and she would name their first daughter.

"I thought she was joking," said the girl's father, James Williams, thirty-three, of Beaumont, where Jameshauwnnel was born.

State registrars had to take parts of seven other birth certificates and glue and staple them into the girl's certificate to make it official. The birth certificate is twenty-one inches long. Mrs. Williams said this was "just as long as she was when she was born."

The name caused so many problems for record-keepers that after the girl was born State Registrar W. D. Carroll issued orders that the state would not accept any names that could not fit on two typewritten lines in the 5⅛-inch space on the official birth certificate. The girl's name is:

Rhoshandiatellyneshiaunneveshenkesciannesha imondrischlyndasaccarnaerenquellenendrasame cashaunettethalemeicoleshiwhalhinive'onchelleca undenesheaalausondrilynnejeanetrimyranaekues aundrilynnezekeriakenvaunetradevonneyavonda latarneskcaevontaepreonkeinesceellaviavelzadaw nefriendsettajessicannelesciajoyvaelloydietteyvet tesparklenesceaundrieaquenttaekatilyaevea'shau wneoraliaevaekizzieshiyjuanewandalecciannerena yeitheliapreciousnesceverroneccaloveliatyroneve kacarrionnehenriettaescecleonpatraruthetiachars alynnmeokcamonaeloiesalynnecsiannemerciadel lesciacustillaparissalondonveshadenequamonec aalexetiozetiaquaniaenglaundneshiafrancethosh aromeshaunnehawaineakowethauandavernellch ishankcarlinaaddoneillesciachristondrafawndreala otrelleoctavionnemiariasarahtashabnequckagail enaxeteshiataharadaponsadeloriakoentescacraig neckadellanierstellavonnemyiatangoneshiadiana corvettinagodtawndrashirlenescekilokoneyashar rontannamyantoniaaquinettesequioadaurilessia quatandamerceddiamaebellecescajamesauwnnel tomecapolotyoajohnyaetheodoradilcyana Koyaan isqatsiuthawyhaiashieakhauwnne Williams.

Robber Has Trouble with Paper Bag Disguise

JACKSONVILLE, FLA. (AP) — Police won't have to collar this suspect—they might try to bag him. And, they say, he would even provide the bag.

They say the robber showed up with a bag on his head to stick up a supermarket in the Jacksonville, Florida, area. A clerk says the bag had eye holes, but the holes had shifted during the robbery, leaving the robber in the dark.

And she says that during the robbery the bag broke open, so she recognized the guy as a regular customer.

Police say they don't know if the man was armed—but he had a bag on one hand, too.

In any case, they say that the paper-bag robber was not sackcessful.

Invitations Sent Out for Monkey Feast

BANGKOK, THAILAND (AP) — The invitations have gone out and hundreds of monkeys are eagerly awaiting their second annual sitdown, courtesy of a local hotel owner.

Yongyoot Kitwattanusoan, the owner of the Lopburi Inn, said Monday he is spending $32,000 to throw the bash—complete with waiters, menus, and napkins—for about six hundred monkeys on Sunday.

Yongyoot offers the meal to thank the monkeys for the success of his hotel in Lopburi, a small provincial capital about seventy miles north of Bangkok. The monkeys, which stay at the Buddhist shrine of Wat Pra Karn, are symbols of good fortune and a prime attraction for tourists.

The hotelkeeper said he sent sixty invitation cards to the monkeys, which grabbed them and leapt back up the shrine.

"We invite all the monkeys to attend a meal party on the occasion of the second anniversary of the Lopburi Inn on Nov. 25 at 10 A.M.," the cards said.

It will be a sitdown affair; that is, if Yongyoot can keep the furry creatures seated at the fifty tables.

"We will serve vegetarian food, including American fried rice, vegetable salad, papaya, various kinds of fruit and dessert," he said in a telephone interview.

"Last year, tens of thousands of people came to see the Lopburi monkeys eat the food we hosted for them," he said.

This year the spread is larger. Yongyoot said that a count by the keepers of the temple found there were 100 more monkeys this year than last.

Number Up for Careless Hong Kong Safecracker

HONG KONG (Reuters) — A Chinese safecracker arrested by Hong Kong police had the combination of a safe he planned to rob written on his arm.

The *Hong Kong Standard* newspaper, quoting police, said the man was one of a gang of three hired in China by a Hong Kong criminal.

Police are studying maps carried by the men to discover where the safe was located.

The Buck Stops Here

BOGOTÁ, COLOMBIA (UPI) — Traveling to Colombia can sometimes cause confusion and hilarity, not because of popular customs and travelers' experiences but because people laugh when they learn of the names villages have chosen for themselves.

Colombian peasants are easy to identify by their clothes and their preference for using common words that are colloquial language not necessarily found in the dictionary.

Many of the names have something to do with a town's routine life. In Tamalameque, a municipality in Bolivar department [state], there exists a town called Pasa Corriendo, or "keep on going."

The peasants show their cunning, too. On the outskirts of Guamal municipality, in Magdalena department, there's a village called A ver si puedo, or "[We'll] see if I can," and another little village in the township of Chiriguana, in César province, is called Hasta aqui llegaste, or "The buck stops here."

Near the city of Valledupar, the capital of César, there is a little town called Asi es la vida, or "That's life." In Colombia they also have the North Pole and the South Pole, but in neither one will you ever find temperatures below zero.

The peasants' imagination apparently has no limits. One town in César is called Paguesepa, or "That'll teach you."

A tourist can also visit Iran, Ireland, Iceland, Hawaii, and the Ukraine without ever leaving Colombia.

The local names never fail to surprise visitors. For instance, a tiny town near the Venezuelan border is called Parate bien, or "Stand up straight!"

Nail Sled

OSLO (AP) — A daredevil here slid down a ski slope while lying on a bed of nails, news reports said.

Inge Vidar Svingen, forty-one, claimed to have survived the run without suffering a puncture.

For the stunt Svingen removed his shirt and lay on the bed of 270 six-inch nails mounted on skis. He then slid five hundred yards down the children's hill of a ski run in southern Norway.

"I am no masochist," Svingen told the local news-

paper, *Dagbladet.* "Abroad I am treated like a big entertainer. Here at home, I'm seen as a half-wit."

Svingen had predicted a sixty-two-m.p.h. top speed, but his device moved slowly.

Car Thieves Nabbed Trying to Steal Undercover Police Van

LAKELAND, FLA. (AP) — Of all the cars and trucks in a local shopping mall's parking lot on one of the year's busiest shopping days, a quartet of would-be car thieves picked on a police surveillance van.

"It was hard to keep from laughing," said Mike Link, one of three officers hiding in the back of the van Saturday when one of the group climbed inside and turned the key.

The would-be thief was grabbed from behind by

a Lakeland police officer and arrested with his buddies.

"He was definitely surprised, because he screamed a lot," said Link.

The van was part of a special unit, including foot patrols and undercover cars, dispatched to the Lakeland Square mall to combat holiday-related parking lot crime.

Undercover officers first spotted the four suspects walking through the lot and flipping up door handles. They approached the van and were about to break in, but too many shoppers were nearby, Link said.

When the thieves moved on to a neighboring strip mall, the police followed in their 1985 Chevrolet van.

This time one of the teenagers got in, turned the key, and was nabbed.

The charges against the four included grand theft and resisting arrest.

Police: Woman Steals Ambulance, Says She Was Late for Work

MIAMI, FLA. (AP) — A woman who said she was late for work stole an ambulance and struck another car before she was stopped, according to authorities.

"I couldn't believe it," said Eduardo Fabregas, who was left by the road Monday with two other paramedics and a patient who had complained of respiratory problems.

"The truck was rolling right away from us," Fabregas said. "I thought it was some other fireman pulling a joke on us, taking it around the corner or something."

The Miami Fire Department ambulance was parked with its motor running when thirty-two-year-old Aurelia Small jumped in and took off, police said.

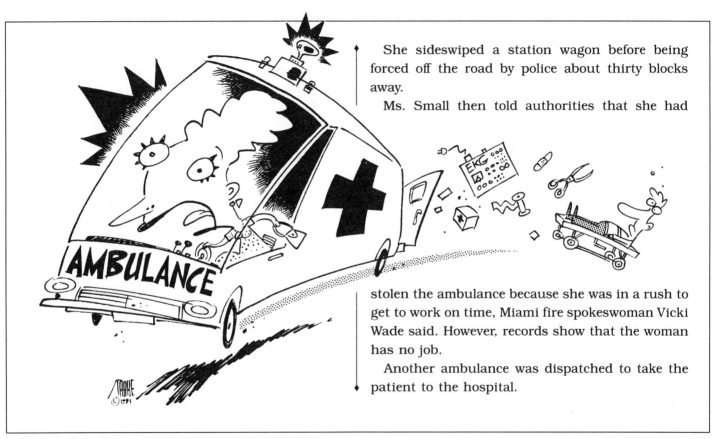

She sideswiped a station wagon before being forced off the road by police about thirty blocks away.

Ms. Small then told authorities that she had stolen the ambulance because she was in a rush to get to work on time, Miami fire spokeswoman Vicki Wade said. However, records show that the woman has no job.

Another ambulance was dispatched to take the patient to the hospital.

A Day in the Life of a Car Thief, Darn it

NEW YORK (Reuters) — The long arm of the law didn't have to reach very far to collar a would-be car thief, New York police say.

A grab across the front seat ended the joyride before the getaway even got going.

Where the miscreant made a mistake—a big one, officers said—was in trying to steal a police car with a policeman in it.

Officer Daniel Daly, who was sitting in the passenger seat of the idling police car, popped handcuffs on the perpetrator after a brief struggle.

Aundray Burns, twenty-six, faces a litany of charges in the incident.

Mayor Wants Legal Ban on Bad Moods

OSLO (AP) — Mayor Arne Nilsen wants to make grumpiness illegal in his island community of Sund.

Nilsen told an Oslo newspaper that he will propose a resolution at a township council meeting requiring five thousand Sund residents to be happy and think positively while banning crankiness.

"Unless the other council members are in a bad mood, I expect a majority in favor," the newspaper *Dagbladet* quoted him as saying.

Sund residents are not abnormally gloomy, but they "get caught up in negative and sad things, rather than seeing all there is to be happy about. I am trying to do something about it," he said.

Irascible islanders will not be prosecuted. But Nilsen said that the lighthearted edict might jolt them into better spirits. The proposal exempts sulkers with good cause, such as the brokenhearted, the report said.

British Eccentrics Alive and Well—And May Live Next Door

LONDON (Reuters) — A British aristocrat named Lucinda wants to offer herself as a virgin sacrifice to an extinct volcano. She takes her pet lobster for walks on a leash and has bought it a yellow crab as a companion.

Lucinda is not alone. One in every ten thousand Britons manifests some degree of eccentricity, according to researcher David Weeks, who disclosed the results of a scientific study of the phenomenon.

Weeks found examples from all walks of life, like a self-styled potato inspector who eats nothing but potatoes, reads books on the vegetable, and goes potato hunting in Peru.

News of the study reached a middle-aged man

living in a cave in the west of Scotland, who offered to serve as a case for Weeks to examine.

Tall and thin, with a bristly moustache and beard and a soft felt hat, the man said he had to vacate the cave at high tide with his two dogs, which were the managing directors of his firm.

A modern-day Robin Hood stalks London parks in green tights and a peaked hat when he is not working as a scientist in a government department. Unlike the medieval folk hero, however, he does not rob the rich to give to the poor.

Compiling the study had its risks. One of Week's assistants visited a man who had installed thirty model tanks on his front lawn and called himself a militarist. The man, answering questions lying in bed, pulled out a grenade from under the covers and asked, "Frightened, dearie?"

The cases include several inventors. One man thought up a hot-air-balloon strategic defense system to blitz radioactivity with laser beams.

There was also the man who enjoyed sailing down tall-storied buildings dressed as a pink elephant, and the doctor who wanted to compile the world's longest history of the enema.

"Blessed are the cracked, because they should let in the light," one elderly woman told Weeks.

Rent-a-Dog

WENGEN, SWITZERLAND (AP) — Rental fee: a dollar per mile. Fuel: dog biscuits.

Hiring a motor vehicle is out in this carfree resort, but a rental canine named General Sam Houston, Jr.—Housty, for short—has become something of a craze for tourists who go walking.

Christian Straessle, who manages his family's four-star hotel, said the shaggy two-year-old dog is a hit, because he adapts easily to all of Wengen's international clientele.

"I always speak Italian with him," said Straessle, a multilingual Swiss. "He also understands German, French, English, and Spanish. Now he's learning Japanese like crazy."

"I need a dog that gets along well with guests and likes kids," said Straessle.

Guests who want to take Housty out usually face a waiting list. The enterprise, launched eighteen months ago, has generated a file of about five hundred customers.

Housty was named after the Texas city where Straessle bought him. The rent-a-dog idea came when Straessle was looking for something catchy to advertise at the hotel reception desk.

Payment of the mileage charge is not enforceable, though people do pay something close to it, said Straessle, who strictly forbids guests from feeding Housty on their own.

"We give them dog cookies to take along. You just can't restrain children, but this way we know how much he eats."

Woman Wins Fight to Keep "Menopoz" License Plates

SEATTLE (AP) — A motorist who wants to end the stigma associated with menopause almost didn't get to keep her personalized license plates that read "MENOPOZ" until a licensing official going through the same rite of passage intervened.

"There's nothing offensive or indecent about menopause," said the motorist, fifty-year-old Dorothy Mitchell. "Even if it's on my license plates."

She was told there had been a complaint and her plates were being canceled.

"It has come to our attention that the phrase used on your personalized plate, MENOPOZ, is offensive to good taste and decency," said the letter from Bob Anderson, Assistant Director of Vehicle Services in the state Department of Licensing.

Under state law, the department can refuse to issue or withdraw such plates, said Anderson, who also sent Mitchell new license plates.

On Friday, however, the state had a change of heart.

"It's time for menopause to come out of the closet," Licensing Director Mary Faulk told Mitchell. "I'm forty-eight and I'm going through it also."

Faulk said she reversed the decision "because I don't think a normal process of aging to be in bad taste."

Mitchell, who works in customer service at a United Parcel Service office, said she got the idea for the MENOPOZ plate after she bought a "dumb, sporty new car" six months ago.

"I bought the car on impulse, and when I told my dad, he wanted to know why I did that because I always have been very conservative," she said. "I told him that it must have been my menopausal phase—and then I thought, I'll put that on my license plate."

Seventh Grader Throws the Book at the World Book

LENOIR, N.C. (AP) — Twelve-year-old Sammy Hicks doesn't have much interest in girls or gym, and the publishers of the *World Book Encyclopedia* probably can't wait until he does.

Sammy reads the encyclopedia—for fun—and as he leafed through his 1990 set recently, he spotted a picture of the Biltmore Estate in Asheville.

Something looked wrong. Sammy had visited there recently and recalled the staircase was on the left side. But there in Volume IX, page 487, was a picture of the staircase—on the right side.

"It's a reasonable mistake," said the seventh grader, who promptly dashed off a note to the Chicago-based encyclopedia publisher. "But you hardly ever find a mistake in the encyclopedia."

The publisher replied, thanking him for the tip and saying the blunder would be corrected in the 1991 edition.

Sammy is also the inventor of bed slippers with headlights, a prize winner in Caldwell County's annual science fair, and enjoys pizza, geometry, outer space and cooking.

Tweaking the *World Book* seems to be another new pastime. When the publisher answered his letter, the reply was addressed to "Sammy Kicks."

"I think I ought to write them another letter," Sammy said.

Battle of the Sexes

Divorce Records

MOUNT CLEMENS, MICH. (AP) — A woman has been ordered to pay her ex-husband $2,800 for damaging his collection of Frank Sinatra platters.

According to court records, Barbara Mossner, forty-one, of Shelby Township was so embittered by her divorce that she damaged the four-hundred-record collection and drew a moustache and glasses on a poster of Ol' Blue Eyes.

Mrs. Mossner, though, said that she took out her anger on the disks before her 1983 divorce from Arthur Mossner. "When he told me he was having an affair, before the divorce was filed, I threw a lot of his records in his den," she said.

Her attorney said Mrs. Mossner considers the $2,800 payout ordered by a circuit court judge a victory. Her husband had valued the collection at $80,000, the lawyer said. The court valued the records at about seven dollars each.

Mrs. Mossner said she'll gladly pay the sum.

"To be perfectly honest, he [Sinatra] was never one of my favorites," she said.*

* Ol' Blue Eyes sent seven music cassettes to Mr. Mossner after reading about the case in a California newspaper. "He got a hoot out of it and wanted to do something for him," said a spokeswoman, Ladonna Keaton.

"I was kind of taken aback. I was thrilled," said Mossner, forty-five. "At least somebody cares....I always figured there is no substitute for class, and that's why I've always been a Sinatra fan."

Soldier Returns from Gulf War to Find His Bottom's a Star

LONDON (Reuters) — A British soldier photographed from behind while taking a shower has returned

from the Gulf War to a hero's welcome. But not the normal sort.

Warren Thompson, twenty-one, was photographed while showering in the Saudi desert, and the picture appeared around the world.

His mother, Andrea Thompson, said dozens of girls impressed with what they saw called to leave their telephone numbers. "I have had loads of calls from girls all over the place, wanting to know all about him," she said.

"I don't know how I'll ever live it down," Thompson said. "I'm so embarrassed."

Doctor Sex

SYRACUSE, N.Y. (AP) — A woman has settled her lawsuit against a former doctor whom she claimed tricked her into having sex by saying it was the best way to administer a secret vaccine.

Both sides agreed not to disclose the amount of the settlement reached Tuesday, said attorney Joseph Fahey, who represented the twenty-one-year- old suburban Syracuse woman. Her lawsuit against Julio Soto of New York City had sought $1.05 million.

Justice Robert J. Nicholson ruled that based on uncontested facts in the case Soto had committed medical malpractice. The state Board of Regents revoked Soto's medical license because of his conduct with the woman, when she was a student at Fordham University.

The woman was suffering from a minor urinary tract infection when Fordham officials referred her to Soto, who was under contract with the school.

Soto admitted to the state Board of Professional Medical Conduct that he lied when he told the woman she was suffering from herpes and that he could obtain a secret vaccine. He told her the most effective way to administer the vaccine was through sexual intercourse.

The woman also is suing Fordham for $4.5 million, claiming that the school was responsible for Soto's conduct. That suit is still pending.

Chinese "Sex Criminals" Needle Women in Shanghai

BEIJING (Reuters) — "Sex criminals" in Shanghai, China's largest city, have sunk to a new low, sticking sewing needles into young women's bottoms on buses, the local Xinmin evening newspaper said.

A twenty-three-year-old woman underwent surgery to remove a four cm- (1.4 inch-) long sewing needle from her thigh.

Bride Wants Annulment, Tells Court "He" Turns Out to Be a She

MEMPHIS, TENN. (UPI) — A teenage girl is suing for annulment of her marriage because her "husband" turned out to be a woman.

A Chancery Court suit filed by the seventeen-year-old girl charges that she was deceived by her nineteen-year-old "husband" and asks that the marriage be voided because "the parties have entered into a homosexual marriage, such a marriage being immoral" according to Tennessee law.

A Memphis minister who counseled the couple for ten hours before marrying them in an elaborate church ceremony last year said the discovery came as a complete shock to the girl, church members, and himself.

"I'm a certified sex therapist," said the minister, who asked that his name be withheld. "I'm not that easily fooled." But he said the groom looked and acted like a man.

"He had masculine characteristics," the minister said. "I learned later that he was taking male hormones."

The clergyman, who had had reservations about marrying the couple anyway, because of their ages, said he agreed only after the girl threatened to run away. Bridal showers were given, invitations sent out, and a formal wedding held.

It was not until after the couple left for a new home in Atlanta that the minister began to hear rumors about the "groom."

The girl said her "husband" told her that he was

deformed because of a football injury and refused to undress in front of her, the minister said.

About four months after the marriage, the girl began having second thoughts when she heard her husband's parents refer to him by a girl's name when she was out of the room, the minister said.

She soon returned to Memphis, where she filed the annulment request.

"Judas Kiss" Costs Adulterous Lover His Tongue

RIO DE JANEIRO (Reuters) — A jealous woman punished her lover in Brazil after she found out he was married by biting off a chunk of his tongue while pretending to kiss him, police said.

"The woman swallowed the piece of tongue to prevent him from having it sewn back on," said a police spokesman in the northeastern city of Salvador.

The attack occurred on Monday night after the woman found out her lover was married, police said.

Djalma José dos Santos, forty-seven, is recovering in the hospital.

"That was a real Judas kiss," the man, unable to speak, wrote on a piece of paper, police said. He was referring to disciple Judas Iscariot's kissing of Jesus Christ after betraying him to the Romans.

The woman has disappeared, police said.

Court to Rule in Rent Row over Rowdy Romps

COLOGNE, GERMANY (AFP) — A Cologne landowner is suing a middle-aged couple who have unilaterally reduced their rent, saying they cannot sleep because their neighbors make too much noise making love, court sources said.

The defendants, both in their fifties, deducted 170 deutschemarks (115 dollars) off their 740 DM (503 dollars) rent after vainly complaining for months about the grunts, squeals, and shouts of encouragement coming through the wall.

The court reserved judgment until an independent assessment of the volume of noise could be made by a bailiff.

Sex on the Roof Is Turkish Delight— Until You Fall Off

ISTANBUL (Reuters) — A Turkish doctor has issued a health warning to people who like to have sex on

the roof of their house. Take care not to fall off.

"Many couples in rural Turkey sleep on the roof on hot summer nights," said brain surgeon Askin Karadayi.

"Some fall off as they slumber, and some fall as they are making love," he told the newspaper *Hurriyet*.

Indonesia Probes Rumors of Fierce Amazon Tribe

JAKARTA (AFP) — Indonesian authorities plan to probe rumors of the existence of a fierce, women-only tribe living near an isolated lake in the easternmost province of Irian Jaya, the news agency Antara said.

Antara quoted the province's social affairs office as saying that a team had been set up last week and was scheduled to leave for the Mamberano subdistrict Tuesday to find out whether the tribe really existed.

A local belief has it that these amazons lived near a lake in the thick jungles on the mountain range of Mamberano.

The amazons were said to capture males from other tribes to beget babies before killing them. All male babies are killed at birth, according to the study.

The government team would carry audiovisual equipment and basic presents such as salt, candies, cigarettes, and foodstuffs, Antara said. It did not say how many women and men were in the seventeen-strong team.

"We'll have to wait for the result of the expedition. . . . They will be able to prove whether a tribe composed of women only exists or that it is merely a legend," an official said.

He pointed out that an expedition went to the

Merauke district and successfully proved the previously rumored existence of an isolated tribe called the Kowaris, whose members live up in trees.

Antipersonals: Big Grudges in Small Print

NEW YORK (AP) — Forget about finding that special someone to share sunsets and fireside chats. If you'd rather find that special moron who bumped you in the checkout line, a weekly shopper has just the ticket: Antipersonals.

Manhattan Pennysaver now invites readers to "give the gift of hate" by placing an advertisement in a special section where people are cut down to size in small print.

"Slay a rotten neighbor. Badmouth the public figure of your choice," the paper urges readers.

"Spew forth your anger. You'll feel much better afterwards."

At a rate of ten dollars for twenty words (fifty cents for each additional word), New Yorkers have been verbally kneecapping each other since the Antipersonals appeared some months ago.

The page offers an opportunity to have the last word in the kind of impersonal yet acrimonious run-ins for which the nation's largest city is famous.

Some examples, occasionally suggesting a casual command of English grammar, spelling, and punctuation:

Attn: The girl who was wearing the tight leopard jump suit with black pumps who purposely stepped on my foot while you was getting off the R train last Wednesday. Meet me at the end of the 63rd Avenue station next Wednesday. I got some shoes with your butt's name on them. —Rita.

To the misery who purposely let the elevator door close while I was standing there with my hands full. Don't be alarmed when the banging noise becomes so great it sounds as though it's coming through your ceiling. Sweet dreams!
—Your Upstairs Neighbor.

To the insensitive boob in the business suit and sneakers who watched me get mugged on the No. 1 train last week without doing a damn thing to help. Pig.

2-13, 2:30 P.M. Downtown No. 2 train—You, light blue rain coat, sunglasses. Me, tall, short blonde hair reading accounting book. Learn some manners!

But most of the Antipersonals deal with that bottomless source of bitterness and disillusion, romance.

One is addressed to the Faxman: "Faxes are impersonal and cold. If the best you could do was fax me your reasons for breaking up, the best I can do is tell you it is over and drop dead in an Antipersonal."

Even casual dates seem to inspire intense recrimination. Many Antipersonals are taken out by women to complain about dates who tried to drive too fast, go too far, or eat too much.

"Dear Jake," writes Janet. "Thanks for the wonderful dinner. . . . After eating with your fingers, burping & passing wind all evening I say, 'Find somebody else to date that's your own species.'"

Man Sentenced Who Dressed Up As Girl and Made Cheerleading Squad

COLORADO SPRINGS, COLO. (AP) — A twenty-six-year-old man who enrolled in a high school as a girl and made the all-girl cheerleading squad was sentenced to two years' probation.

El Paso County District Judge Richard Hall said

Charles Daugherty must continue counseling and stay out of trouble with the law as conditions of that probation.

Daugherty had been diagnosed earlier as having multiple personalities. He told Hall at one hearing that he wants to get a high school diploma and become a psychologist.

Daugherty pleaded guilty on Jan. 3 to criminal impersonation and could have been sentenced to up to two years in jail.

He enrolled at Coronado High School on Sept. 6 as a junior under the name of Cheyen (pronounced Shawn) Weatherly.

The ruse was detected eight days later after school officials became suspicious and began checking his records. Daugherty had claimed to be a transfer student from Greece and had given school officials computer records that proved to be false.

In the meantime, several football players had expressed interest in dating the newest member of the cheerleading squad, despite Daugherty's solid build: he is five feet nine and 164 pounds.

He performed in uniform with the cheerleading squad at a pep assembly and changed clothes in the women's locker room, students and teachers say.

When Daughtery's masquerade came to light, several girls who had befriended the new cheerleader were upset, but some said they had had their doubts all along.

"He had a lot of makeup on. It looked like it was plastered. He had makeup where his beard would be," a sixteen-year-old classmate said at the time.

Court Allows Woman to Beat Husband Before Granting Divorce

BORSAD, INDIA (AP) — A local court permitted a woman to publicly beat her husband before it granted him a divorce, United News of India reported.

The beating occurred Oct. 7 but went unreported until a social organization, apparently outraged by the incident, complained to the government. No further action has been taken.

The man, from a town in the western Gujarat state, was seeking a divorce from his first wife to marry another woman, the news agency reported. She agreed, on condition that he first submit to a beating.

Under Indian law, Hindus can have only one wife at a time. The law does not apply to Moslems, who are permitted up to four wives.

Gujarat is the home state of Mohandas K. Gandhi, who led India's struggle for freedom against English rule and preached *ahimsa*, or nonviolence.

Women Protest Light Sentence for Condom Rapist

LONDON (Reuters) — Women's rights groups reacted angrily to a British judge's decision to give a rapist a light sentence because he showed consideration toward his victim by wearing a condom.

Judge Arthur Myerson sentenced Brian David Huntley to only three years in prison after Huntley admitted raping a nineteen-year-old prostitute in Hull, in northeast England.

"You showed concern and consideration by wearing a contraceptive," the judge told Huntley.

Myerson told the court that prostitutes were a vulnerable group who were often treated with contempt and said the woman had not suffered long-term effects.

But a spokeswoman for the group Women Against Rape called for the judge's dismissal.

"We think the judge's remarks are outrageous. He is preventing women getting justice. Whether the attacker was wearing a condom has nothing to do with it," spokeswoman Claire Glasman said.

New and Improved

From Ooze Balls to Boinks

PHILADELPHIA (AP) — The Rooter-Tooter, which is handy for heckling referees, and a mug that melts as you drink from it are two of the weird and wacky gadgets inventors hope will become the latest fads.

More than thirty inventors from around the country recently converged on the "Fad Fair" at the Franklin Institute Science Museum. There they showed off such goofy gizmos as decorative noses, balls made of ooze, and bicycle helmets with three-dimensional funny faces.

The fair was organized by Ken Hakuta, better known as Dr. Fad to viewers of a local children's television show.

Hakuta is also the inventor of the Wacky Wallcrawler. If you throw the sticky, octopus-like toy against a wall, it crawls down by itself. It has helped Hakuta walk off with more than $20 million over the past eight years, he says.

Most of the inventions on display need backers. Hakuta predicted that ten of them would be marketed and two would make money. But that doesn't discourage inventors.

"These are the eternal optimists," he said.

Craig Boyko, of Fairfield, Iowa, came to the Fad Fair with two idiosyncratic inventions. One is the Ooze Ball, made of a substance that stretches, bounces, and makes popping sounds. The other is the Bite Lite, a tiny, furry creature with teeth that can grasp a child's clothing and light the way with a flashlight it carries in its tail. Great for kids who are afraid of the dark.

Boyko's first invention was the Zube Tube, a three-foot cylinder that makes weird noises when people yell through it. About 1 million have been sold since 1989.

Inventor Saul Freedman arrived at the fair with hopes of marketing his ice mug, a molded container that melts away after the liquid inside is consumed. Freedman, of Vineland, New Jersey, designed the mug after discovering that many coastal communities don't allow beverages on the beach, because of the cups and bottles left behind. With Freedman's ice mug, all that remains is a small wooden handle.

Also up for grabs is the All-American Rooter-Tooter, which issues an obnoxious sound like a Bronx cheer. Inventor Robert Gastel, of Mission, Texas, designed the horn after disagreeing with the calls referees made at a Dallas Cowboys–Washington Redskins football game.

The fair's guest of honor was Betty James, coinventor of the granddaddy of all wacky toys, the Slinky, first marketed in 1945. Her husband, Richard James, got the idea for the toy when he saw a coil fall off a machine at the Philadelphia Naval Yard.

IT'S WACKY!
IT'S WEIRD!
IT'S GOOEY!
IT'S OOZE-BALL

Volkswagen Unveils Parking Heaven: Look Ma! No Hands!

NEW YORK (AP) — The old Volkswagen Beetle had one big advantage in parking—it was small. But a new Volkswagen concept car goes a long step beyond that: it parks itself.

Researchers at the world's number four car maker have developed a "look Ma, no hands" parking system that can do it all, even parallel park.

Volkswagen officials and media doubters gathered in Central Park for a demonstration of the automatic parking system in Volkswagen's Integrated Research Futura concept car.

The sleek, gull-wing car was driven out of its parking spot by a Volkswagen engineer. At the point when most drivers begin craning their necks and twisting their bodies into unnatural positions, he simply got out.

With a push of a button the steering wheel turned and the car moved backward, forward, backward, and forward again until it was neatly parked a hairsbreadth from the curb.

Heiko Barske, head of research for the Volkswagen Group, joked that "the next generation of car will be able to drive itself—and the driver can just stay home."

Chinese Restauranteur Stuffed Buns with Human Flesh

BEIJING (AFP) — Wang Guang's restaurant in the central Chinese province of Sichuan was making a fortune serving buns stuffed with a spicy filling—until authorities discovered that the stuffing was made of human flesh.

Mr. Wang's brother, who worked in a crematorium, supplied him with the "thighs and buttocks from corpses," which were ground and heavily spiced Sichuan-style, the regional publication *News Digest* said.

Steamed buns are often stuffed with pork in China.

Mr. Wang sold his creations at unbeatable prices and had to work hard to satisfy demand, the report said.

He was able to save the equivalent of $6,000 in a few years, a small fortune in the Chinese economy, it said.

His secret was discovered when the family of a young woman who had died wanted to see the body before it was cremated. The parents were shocked to see that their daughter's thighs and buttocks had been removed, the *News Digest* said.

Authorities soon figured out the connection but were divided on how to charge the two brothers: with theft, defiling the dead, abusing the trust of clients, or shady business practices.

Japanese Women Prepare for Summer with Bug-resistant Pantyhose

Tokyo (Reuters) — Can you say "ants in your pants" in Japanese?

New bug-resistant pantyhose, the latest rage in Japan, means you won't have to.

With miniskirts back in fashion and summer on the way, fastidious Japanese women are stepping out and snapping up the latest in underwear: "insecticide pantyhose."

A spokesman for the Kanebo textile and cosmetics firm said that it had already sold more than 400,000 pairs of the pantyhose since they went on sale.

"Of course, sales volume is nowhere near that for regular pantyhose," said the spokesman. "But considering this product's extraordinary character, it's been selling very well."

The chemical with which the garments are impregnated is harmless for humans, he said, but lethal for the spiders and cockroaches that increasingly infest offices in Japan's carpeted, air-conditioned tower blocks.

Urinal for Women Unveiled at Chicago Trade Show

Chicago (Reuters) — A urinal designed for women who prefer not to sit on public toilet seats was unveiled at a trade show on Friday.

Called the She-inal, the device resembles the traditional urinal used by men except for its gooseneck hose and funnel.

"A handle on the funnel allows women to adjust it to the proper position and height," said the manufacturer, Urinette, Inc., of Pensacola, Florida.

"Clothing need only be moved a few inches out of the way. When finished, the user simply rehangs the funnel on the hook inside the unit and flushes. Hovering and covering are no longer necessary," it said.

The company said that studies show that up to 98 percent of women do not sit on public toilet seats, "preferring hovering, covering (with paper), or heading for home." The She-inal, unlike its male counterpart, is designed for use in private individual stalls.

Tell 'em Charlie Sent Ya

Florida Bar Serving Goldfish Finds Itself In Fishbowl

FORT LAUDERDALE, FLA. (Reuters) — Some bars have patrons who drink like fish. One bar in Fort Lauderdale has customers who drink fish.

At the Everglades Bar patrons can down a wriggling goldfish in their shot of tequila, peppermint schnapps, or Grand Marnier.

Manager Mike Sill said Thursday that the strange practice began as a joke and no one paid much attention for well over a year, while the bar went through about three dozen goldfish a week.

Then a patron complained, and the bar found itself and its goldfish in a fishbowl.

First the police came, but the officer was laughing so hard he could barely fill out his report, Sill said. Then the local television cameras appeared. Now the health department is on the scene.

But serving goldfish isn't against the law, Sill said. The health department said only that the pub must acquire the fish "from an approved source," and Sill has already received calls from several potential suppliers.

In the meantime, he said, he is serving goldfish crackers.

Dancing Dinners

TOKYO (AP) — The latest in food rages in Japan is to eat fish live—flounder that flap around on the plate, finger-length eel swallowed raw. And remember, if the shrimp don't dance, send 'em back.

"The food moves around a lot—that's the whole idea," said Sunao Uehara, a chef at Chunagon, a well-known seafood restaurant in the Ginza, one of Tokyo's most expensive nightspots.

Shrimp, flounder, and lobster are by no means the only energetic entrees on the trendy diners' menu. Other attractions include firefly squid, loaches, sea bream, and young yellowtail.

When the waiters bring the fish in, the fish are wiggling, their eyes and mouths moving. Then they quickly slice open the fish's midsection and gut it, so the fish is ready to eat. Like sushi or sashimi, the slices are dipped in a mixture of soy sauce and horseradish.

Lobster is served belly up, with an incision made along the length of the tail so diners can get at the meat. Small squid and eels are eaten whole.

Shrimp are featured in a dish called dance, and they are expected to do just that.

"We're packing them in," boasted Uehara, who personally specializes in preparing live lobster.

Though some Japanese express misgivings about eating live food, it is a concept that fits in easily with the emphasis on freshness and *au naturel* presentation upon which Japanese gastronomy is based.

Toshio Fujii, an X-ray technician from a stretch of Japan's western coast where discerning seafood eaters are the rule, said he prefers to eat his fish live because "they don't come any fresher. My seven-year-old daughter likes them, too," he said. "But eels are kind of gross. I had them in my beer one time. Too many little bones."

I've Fallen and I Can't Get Up

Swarming Bees Drive Owner Out of Car, Close Car Wash

BATON ROUGE, LA. (AP) — Maddie Mix's lunchtime stop at the car wash turned into a three-hour ordeal when a swarm of bees commandeered her newly scrubbed car.

"I just said, 'Why me, Lord?' I've got so much stuff to do," Mix said as she watched thousands of bees buzz in and out of her Buick.

Gene Humphreys, who owns Hammond Aire Auto Spa, said the first bees landed on the car as it headed into his one-hundred-foot-long wash tunnel.

"When we drove it in through the tunnel, there must have been one hundred bees on the door," he said. "We blasted them off with the hose . . . it wasn't ten minutes there must have been ten thousand bees all over it. They massed so big you couldn't see the color of her car. The interior of her car was black with bees. The ceiling of her car was black with bees."

The swarm forced him to close the car wash for more than two hours, until a beekeeper from Louisiana State University could remove the swarm.

Humphreys said the bees were "hitting me like raindrops, they were coming at me in such masses."

"I thought they were killer bees," said Beau Michael, who drove the car through the car wash. He was the only person who got stung—he sat on a bee while moving the car.

Terry Tillman, a former beekeeper who drove into the car wash just as the bees landed, and the LSU beekeeper said the bees apparently were confused because they couldn't find their queen.

Humphreys said the beekeeper lured most of the bees into a trap filled with honeycomb.

Ms. Mix wound up leaving her car at the car wash and getting a ride back to work before the bees were all removed.

Humphreys had a series of photographs of the swarm. "I gave Maddie . . . some of the best of them. She said, 'I know my boss won't believe me if I say that's why I was late to work,'" he said.

Ninety-Nine-Year-Old Dutchman Survives Hospital Leap

AMSTERDAM (Reuters) — A ninety-nine-year-old heart patient survived after jumping out of a third-floor hospital window and crashing through a tiled roof below, officials said.

They said the patient had apparently tired of being treated in the intensive care unit, smashed the window, and jumped out. He was not seriously hurt and was put back in bed.

Dog Bites Buffalo, Buffalo Gores Indian Priest to Death

NEW DELHI (Reuters) — A rabid dog bit a buffalo, which went berserk and trampled several people before goring to death a Brahmin priest conducting a cremation service, the United News of India reported.

The agency said a veterinary surgeon in the south India state of Tamil Nadu put down the buffalo with an injection. It did not say what happened to the dog.

Velcro-Suited Drinkers Hooked on Madcap New Zealand Pub Game

NAPIER, NEW ZEALAND (Reuters) — New Zealanders dressed in Velcro suits are bounding off a mini-trampoline and sticking themselves to a Velcro-covered wall in the latest madcap sport to hook drinkers at a small town pub.

"The aim of the game is for people to race up and splat themselves on the wall with their feet as high off the ground as possible," pub owner Jeremy Bayliss said.

Bayliss told Reuters that the latest craze had been inspired by the U.S. space program. NASA had used suits made of the sticky fabric Velcro to train astronauts for weightlessness.

The Velcro wall is padded, and so far there have been no injuries. Workers are ready to catch any rebounds, but in most cases contestants stick so hard they have to be peeled off.

The record height of fifteen feet was set by one contestant who did a flip to land face down and feet up.

The suits—one male and one female—cost $1,000 each and the Velcro wall $400.

Driver, Seventy, Flunks Test in Big Way

LOS ANGELES (Reuters) — A seventy-year-old man taking a driving test drove his car through the wall of a Department of Motor Vehicles building yesterday, injuring six office workers and causing $40,000 worth of damage.

"He really flunked that driving test," said police officer Dennis Smith.

The man, who was not named, was taking his test in a DMV parking lot in the Los Angeles suburb of Canoga Park when his car crashed through the wall of the building.

It then careened through the counter area and came to rest in the middle of the office, thirty feet inside the building, Officer Smith said.

Startled office workers scrambled to get out of the car's path, but six did not make it, he said.

Two were treated at the scene for minor injuries and four were taken to a nearby hospital. None of the injuries was serious. The driver of the car was unhurt.

Briton Run over by Own Car After Reporting It Stolen

LONDON (Reuters) — A Briton was run over by his own car moments after leaving a police station where he had reported it stolen.

Richard Weston, twenty-three, of Nottingham, in central England, stepped out of the police station and saw his car waiting at a traffic light. He ran in front of the vehicle to stop it, but the thieves accelerated, hurling him into the air.

Weston was treated at a hospital for internal injuries. The car thieves got away.

Beam Me Up

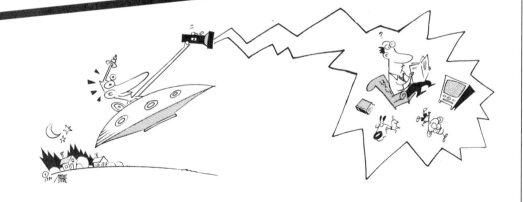

Convention Organizer Says UFOs No Joke

EUREKA SPRINGS, ARK. (AP) — The annual convention of UFO enthusiasts that just ended was no laughing matter, an organizer said.

Lou Farish said he's heard the snickers of people who don't take seriously talk of cow mutilations, crop circles, and extraterrestrial kidnappings. And he insisted it's no joke: space aliens that visit the Soviet Union really do look different than those that visit the United States.

"I'm assuming the skeptics don't know anything about the subject or they don't want to face the implications of the subject. They don't want their world disturbed," Farish said in a telephone interview from the third Ozark UFO Conference.

"The implication of the subject . . . is we're definitely not alone. I don't know if we're in danger.

There's that possibility," said the fifty-three-year-old part-time postal clerk who publishes a news-clipping service about UFOs.

Speakers from around the world gave presentations about UFOs at the conference, which about four hundred people attended.

Sergei Bulantsev, forty-six, a UFO researcher from the Soviet Union, told conferencegoers that aliens in his country are better looking than those in the United States.

"They're just like Europeans, like foreign tourists," Bulantsev said of the aliens that visit the Soviet Union. "It seems to be different teams of aliens are operating in our two countries."

Extraterrestrials Kidnap Peasant

BOGOTÁ, COLOMBIA (AFP) — A Colombian peasant claimed on Colombian radio and television Thurs-

day that he was kidnapped by extraterrestrials and taken 450 kilometers away in a UFO.

Luis Roberto Rodriguez, age fifty-seven, said he was attracted by a strange light at twilight Tuesday as he was leaving his home, located in Tenjo, 40 kilometers north of Bogotá. The light drew him toward a spacecraft three meters high and three meters wide.

Rodriguez, who was riding a horse, abandoned his mount and tried to run away, but he said he was paralyzed.

According to Rodriguez, the interior of the UFO was shaped like a beer bottle. He said there were ◆

three metallic yellow colored beings on board who communicated with him by telepathy.

The UFO took him on a ride, he said, but he doesn't know how long it lasted, because he blacked out.

Rodriguez says he reappeared on Thursday, completely dehydrated, near Pitalito, a village southeast of Huila (450 kilometers from his point of departure), where he was found by a peasant.

Chinese Plane Chases UFO

BEIJING (Reuters) — Passengers on a Chinese domestic flight were treated to an unusually hair-raising flight earlier this week when their plane chased a UFO for nine minutes over China's biggest city, Shanghai, the local Xinmin *Evening News* said.

The oval unidentified flying object, which was larger than the aircraft, flew above Shanghai's Hongqiao Airport before it turned suddenly, rushed toward the plane, and disappeared above it, the newspaper said.

Earthlings, Venusians Discuss Flying Saucers, Elvis

TUCSON (AP) — Omnec Onec, who landed here from Chicago, says life on her native planet, Venus, isn't all that different from life on Earth.

"It's like the desert areas here. It's amazing how adaptable the human species is," said Ms. Onec, one of thirty speakers at the world UFO convention that landed here this month.

The conference drew about four hundred people to a Tucson hotel and included speakers from fourteen countries—and, uh, elsewhere—plus exhibits and copious amounts of literature for sale.

Elvis: The UFO Connection and *Why They Need Us, We Don't Need Them* were among the available books, along with "Beamship Trainee" bumper stickers, "UFOs are Real" baseball caps, and UFO yo-yos.

The lecture subjects included the appearance of mysterious crop circles in England, underground UFO bases in the United States, cow abductions in Missouri, and the kidnapping of witness Paula Watson of Mount Vernon, Mo.

Ms. Watson described how she was canning in her basement, about seven years ago, when she

noticed a silvery alien with large eyes staring at her through a window, after she had witnessed a cow abduction by aliens earlier in the day.

Ms. Watson said she called out to the alien, who backed off, but she went to sleep and awoke on a spaceship. "I was standing up on a white table and the . . . alien was running his hands down my body, scanning my body," she said.

Participants tired by exhibits and lectures could relax at a bar with a Martian martini or mingle with participants claiming unearthly ties.

Ms. Onec, who in her Earth life lives in Chicago and is known as Sheila Gipson, said she is from Teutonia, Venus, where her kind live in the astral plane, as opposed to the physical.

"I lowered my vibrations to be able to come to Earth and pay off a debt I owed to a girl in a previous lifetime—a karmic debt," she said.

Hair Today, Gone Tomorrow

Artist Makes Hair Come Alive

HARRISBURG, PA. (AP) — Tim Bowman sat patiently almost three hours while his shoulder-length mane was sculpted into an elaborate replica of a Three Mile Island cooling tower.

Bowman, a college freshman who lived in the area twelve years ago during the nation's worst nuclear power accident, was a man with a bouffant to die for and a whole evening ahead of him.

The only question: just how to get to sleep after it was all over.

Artist Terry Niedzialek assured him that a couple of shampoos would bring the hairy headpiece tumbling down whenever he decided it was time to become nuclear-free. "You spray it with water to soften it up and then work backwards to remove the pieces. It takes about two shampoos," she said.

Niedzialek, a former New York hairstylist who now resides in eastern Pennsylvania, has been working artistic wonders with hair since about 1983. Her manes with a message portray political, environmental, and technological themes.

At a recent appearance at Harrisburg Area Community College Niedzialek created "Radiation Free" on Bowman's head, featuring a silver cooling tower with a plume of cottony smoke, tree branches draped with green hair, a small plastic cow, and the ultimate wave—a splash from the Susquehanna River that jutted out from the base of his neck.

"I always meant to do a hair montage of a nuclear reactor," she said.

"Oh, wow," said Bowman when he finally glimpsed his new do. "It's huge. It's wonderful. I like it. When I move my head, it feels big. It's hard to describe."

Niedzialek's other designs have depicted the Berlin Wall, war, American politics, and patriotism. In her designs, hair is stretched into asphalt roadways, curled around skyscrapers, woven through factories, flattened by wire cages, and dotted with bulldozers, plastic animals, and toy soldiers.

"It's kind of like whatever strikes me at the time," Niedzialek said. "I wanted what was said in the piece to relate to any nuclear reactor, themes like us versus technology, humanity versus technology," she said.

The artist's creations, some done on wigs, cost from $125 to $3,000.

As for Bowman's new do, the cost would be "the worth of his head," she said.

Sticky Situation

FORT LAUDERDALE, FLA. (AP) — The never-ending quest for "big hair" created with the help of spray has raised a cloud of controversy as middle-school students smuggle in the contraband cosmetic.

About a third of Broward County's twenty-nine middle schools prohibit hair spray on campus, but students say hard-core users are still smuggling it in.

"They're constantly in the bathroom with hair spray," said Christine Selvaggi, a seventh-grader at Seminole Middle School in Plantation. "Some kids complained, because it leaves a terrible smell in there. We're really not supposed to, but everybody brings it in anyway."

"I think it's really unfair because, you know, the teachers at our school, they're not really interested in making themselves up or whatever," eighth-grader Shelley Kuntzman said of the ban, which began at Seminole this school year.

"I spend thirty minutes doing my hair. If you don't get to spray it to where it will hold, there's no point in doing it in the morning before school," Shelley said. She uses a nonaerosol spray, because it's not harmful to the environment. But it also doesn't hold as well, so she needs to spray more often. Twice the physical education teacher at Seminole has taken away her bottles, she said.

Seminole students have lots of theories about the ban. "If someone lights a cigarette in the bathroom, plus the hair spray, it kind of like explodes," seventh-grader Anika Omphroy said.

Hairdressers Upset at Salon's Topless Scheme

ADELAIDE, AUSTRALIA (AFP) — Hairdressers vowed to prevent a hairdressing salon here from offering topless service.

Bill Peacock, president of South Australia's Hairdressers and Cosmetologists Employer's Association, said the salon "would degrade the whole industry."

"What would happen if the girls get molested on the job, or they spill some particular hair products on their nipples, or they cut themselves?" Mr. Peacock said.

A suburban salon advertised for a qualified apprentice hairdresser prepared to work topless, saying it was "an equal opportunity employer."

A spokesman said about ten women and one man had expressed interest in the positions, but the man was told his services were not required. He said the topless service would be available only to adults during restricted hours and a hands-off rule would be enforced.

Big Hair Makes It Big in a Big Hair Town

BALTIMORE (AP) — Anywhere else, it might have seemed like a blast from the past, a trip back to the sixties, a celebration of hair, beautiful hair. But in Baltimore it wasn't that much out of place.

Some of Baltimore's biggest hair turned out Saturday night for the first Hair Ball.

Six hundred people paid fifteen dollars each to benefit the Maryland Art Place gallery. While most just came to admire the hair-based art and live hairdressing demonstrations, many came outrageously coiffed.

"Baltimore is the hairdo capital of the world," said filmmaker John Waters, a Baltimore resident whose films featuring the late Divine, an obese cross-dresser, celebrated Baltimore's craving for coiffures. One of his films is called *Hairspray*.

"The Hair Ball hits a nerve. People get the joke here immediately," he said.

Why Baltimore? In some neighborhoods, beehives and blue tint just never went out of style. When tackiness became a self-conscious fashion statement, Baltimore was suddenly chic.

"Did you know that Baltimore was voted the tackiest city in America? You should be proud of that," said partygoer Gay Pinder. She didn't know who had voted Baltimore the tackiest city honor, but few at the Hair Ball would dispute it.

"Baltimore is such a hair capital," said Charlotte Cohen, the Maryland Art Place program director. "I saw someone today at Lexington Market. She had big hair, big hair."

The bigger the better, said Waters. "Look around. See who's tallest."

Joan Portzman, a bartender and farmer, wore her red hair in a style called "The Flame," which took nine hours of gelling, gluing, and spraying to create. Like a flame, the big, pointy construction leaped into the air.

Hairstylist Lola Jones, who runs the salon where Portzman got fixed up, won a hairdressing competition with a beehive that had artificial bees woven in.

Women weren't the only ones on display. Richard Gorelick, who works in media relations at another gallery, went to a salon to get his hair braided. Instead, he ended up looking like the wrong end of a turkey. "The woman who was cutting my hair wouldn't let me see what she was doing," he said.

Local artists displayed pieces about or containing hair. Jann Rosen-Queralt's "Hair Balls on the Half-Shell" was made of hair, tennis balls, and plastic shells, and Jonathan West's "Bagels and Locks" appeared to be made of bagels, cream cheese, and hair.

Beards Provoke Political Wrath in Moslem Bangladesh

DHAKA, BANGLADESH (Reuters) — Men with beards, a symbol of piety in overwhelmingly Moslem Bangladesh, are at risk from their whiskers in the tumult of the country's transition to democracy.

Since the fall of former president Mohammad Ershad, who provoked a controversy in 1988 by making Islam the state religion, more than a dozen men have been assaulted for no other reason than having beards.

Some were pulled from buses and beaten by students. Others had their whiskers yanked out. Several needed hospital treatment.

One of the victims was an elderly schoolteacher who came to Dacca on a private visit. Others included students, businessmen, and government employees.

Police agree with comments by many Bangladeshi newspapers that the attacks were mostly carried out by supporters of the Awami League party, which was in the forefront of the campaign to oust Ershad.

"People having beards are often mistaken for members or supporters of the fundamentalist Jamaat-e-Islam party or its student front, the Islamic Chhatra Shibir," one police officer said.

Commenting on the issue of the beard and the ballot, the right-wing *Meillat* newspaper asked, "Is this what we call politics?"

Said another newspaper, "The list of so many things we need to protect now includes the most innocent beard."

Prickly Problems

Close Shave Gets Nurse the Sack

MILAN (AFP) — A Milan clinic sacked a nurse after accusing her of deliberately stimulating erections in two men while shaving them for an operation, the nurse said Saturday.

Mrs. W. Bo, fifty-four, who has been in the nursing profession for twenty years, said she received a letter from the Sant' Ambrogio clinic dismissing her for "deliberately provoking an erection in two patients while getting them ready for an operation and for having added to their embarrassment by making the fact public."

Mrs. Bo said that when she had told surgeons about the erections she was merely obeying rules requiring her to report "all significant details about the patient's condition."

Mrs. Bo said she would fight the dismissal in the courts and has been promised full trade union support.

Jury Finds Doctor Not Liable in Penis Implant Suit

FORT LAUDERDALE, FLA. (Reuters) — A jury has ruled that a Fort Lauderdale doctor did not botch a penis implant that left the patient's penis tilting ninety degrees to the right.

"We never said he didn't have a problem," de-fense attorney Ronald Josepher said. "But it was scar tissue, not the doctor's error."

The six-member Broward Circuit Court jury returned the verdict Wednesday evening after a week-long trial.

The plaintiff, Robert Martinique, who is in his early forties, complained of "right angulation," pain, and inability to have sex. He had a penile implant in 1987.

Martinique said that one doctor told him he risked having his penis explode if he tried to have sex.

He later had a second operation to correct the problem, using a smaller implant. Penile implants are mechanical or inflatable devices used by impotent men to achieve sexual intercourse.

The defense argued successfully that the patient suffered unusual, but not unheard of, side effects involving scar tissue formation that were not the fault of the defendant, urologist Dr. Ran Abrahamy.

Tonic Foods Are Winter Favorites in Taiwan

TAIPEI, TAIWAN (Reuters) — On a chilly winter day a group of men sit sweating inside the crowded Chungli Bull House, a restaurant famous for dishes made from the organs of bulls. They are having penis soup.

"It tastes like chicken," said a middle-aged businessman, his face reddened by the Chinese herbs and wine in the soup. "I feel stronger and healthier drinking this in the winter."

Chiang Chun-ho, the owner of the restaurant, said he had consulted several Chinese herbal doctors to create the special recipe, which includes bull testicles and penises and a dozen types of herbs boiled with rice wine.

In addition to increasing sexual potency, the soup is meant to strengthen the overall health of people who drink it. "It doesn't only help men," Chiang said. "It is also good for women and boys."

Seal kidneys, toad ovaries, and the internal organs of snakes are all consumed as tonic foods.

The kidneys help men "perform better." The ovaries improve a woman's skin. The snake organs are believed to increase resistance to disease.

An old Chinese saying runs, "Make up one part by eating the part."

If a man is not sexually potent, for example, eating bull or deer penis is said to help. More controversial, however, is the notion that if a child is not intelligent eating pig's brain will make him or her smarter.

Because of their reputation and scarcity—some animals are protected under conservation laws— the most exotic tonic foods command high prices. A pot of bull-penis soup costs about seventy-five dollars.

Jealous Hong Kong Wife Cuts Off Part of Husband's Penis with Scissors

HONG KONG (Reuters) — A thirty-eight-year-old Hong Kong woman, enraged by her husband's infidelity, snipped off part of his penis with scissors while he slept and flushed it down the toilet, police said.

The thirty-five-year-old man, who was not identified, awoke in agony to find that his wife had attacked him with the scissors because she was jealous of his girlfriend, police said.

He called police before making his way to a nearby clinic.

"About one inch (2.5 cm) was cut off and flushed away," a police spokesman said.

The woman was to appear in court, accused of malicious wounding.

Furry Penis Caused Her Stress, Australian Woman Says

ADELAIDE, AUSTRALIA (Reuters) — An Australian woman is seeking compensation for stress caused by a furry penis that a female colleague kept in their office.

The unnamed woman alleges that she and her husband were made physically and mentally ill by the toy, a Christmas present, which was left on the top of a filing cabinet near her colleague's desk in February 1989.

Since leaving work in August 1989, the public servant has received $10,800 in rehabilitation expenses, including counseling, membership in a gymnasium, and money for an interior decorating course.

Her husband, the office supervisor, has already won $34,000 in benefits for anxiety and depression.

At a hearing of the Administrative Appeals Tribunal in Adelaide this week, the wife asked the tribunal to overturn an earlier rejection of her claim for sickness benefits.*

The owner of the toy said that most people who saw it either asked what it was or laughed.

Witnesses said that another sex toy called Boris, whose genitals were exposed when his beard was lifted, had been sitting in the office for many months without complaints being laid.

* The Administrative Appeals Tribunal rejected the claim, upholding a decision by the federal workers' compensation scheme not to pay sickness benefits.

Bangladeshi Woman Cuts Off Lover's Penis

DHAKA, BANGLADESH (Reuters) — A Bangladeshi woman cut off her lover's penis after he refused to marry her, police said.

Nasima Begum, thirty-five, walked into a police station with the severed organ and told officers that her lover had refused to get married after living with her for eight years.

"I wanted to punish the betrayer and teach a lesson to others like him," she was quoted as saying.

Begum pulled out a knife while she and victim Ashgar Ali were making love one night, according to doctors treating Ali.

Police arrested Begum, but gave no details of the charges she would face.

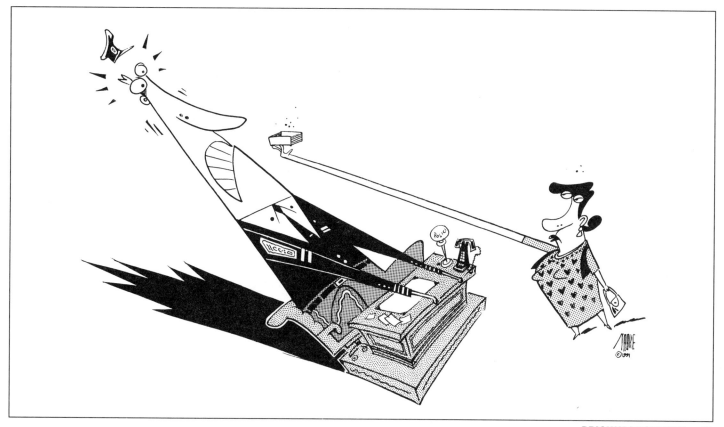

Italian Males Tickled, Then Deflated at News on Condom Sizes

ROME (Reuters) — Italy was rocked Friday by the news that its men needed bigger condoms than other Europeans, but truth later punctured this myth of the Latin lover.

Morning newspapers said that Health Ministers Francesco de Lorenzo had ruled that the smallest regulation size for condoms sold in Italy was larger than in other European countries.

"At least Italy is maxi in something," the usually staid Milan newspaper *Il Giornale* trumpeted in a front-page editorial, and innuendoes about virility packed other newspapers.

Standards for condoms, fixed months ago but unnoticed until parliamentarian Umberto Corsi put a tongue-in-cheek question to de Lorenzo this week, area at least 6.3 inches long by 1.9 inches in diameter.

A ministry statement later Friday said, however, that this was a standard European Community size. Italy had originally set the width at 0.08 inches larger, but backtracked when it realized it exceeded the EC standard.

Meanwhile, *Il Giornale* had asked the minister to reveal if he had a secret dossier on Italian male anatomy, while L'Unita, the newspaper of the former Communist party, worried that foreign tourists might suffer an inferiority complex and feel compelled to bring their own condoms.

We Are Family

Japanese "Dead Man" Walks in As Funeral Is About to Start

Tokyo (Reuters) — An elderly Japanese woman busy making funeral plans got the shock of her life when her son walked into the house seventeen hours after police and relatives pronounced him dead, police said.

Police found a body, apparently a hit-and-run victim, on a road near the family home in Gunman Prefecture, north of Tokyo.

They contacted the old woman's family, who identified the body as her fifty-five-year-old son.

Later it transpired that the son had been staying

at a friend's house and had rushed home when he heard from a neighbor that he was "dead."

Police said they had resumed efforts to establish the identity of the corpse.

Chinese Disguise

BEIJING (Reuters) — A Chinese peasant couple forced their daughter to live like a man for twenty-five years, and even married her off—to a mentally retarded woman—a local newspaper said.

After losing two baby boys, the parents, obsessed with having a male heir, disguised their third baby as a boy, the Qinghai *Daily* said.

The woman, from south China's Hunan Province, tried to commit suicide over her plight before being rescued by local officials, the newspaper said.

She is now married to a man.

Daughter Finds Birth Mother Is Coworker

ROANOKE, VA. (AP) — A daughter's search for the woman who had given birth to her twenty-two years ago ended at the convenience store where she works, when she discovered that she had been working alongside her mother for six months.

Tammy Harris, who was adopted at age two, searched for her natural mother for a year before discovering it was her friend at work, Joyce Schultz.

Three weeks ago, Ms. Schultz, forty-four, overheard Ms. Harris complaining about the difficulty of getting information about her natural parents.

Ms. Harris brought out her birth certificate, and Ms. Schultz, who had been looking for her children, knew she had found her daughter. Afraid to say anything, she asked Ms. Harris for a baby picture. The picture of the little girl matched the pictures Ms. Schultz had of her own daughter.

Ms. Schultz still didn't say anything for days, explaining, "I was frightened she might not like me."

But Ms. Harris, who wondered why her coworker had asked for the baby picture, eventually asked Ms. Schultz point blank, "Are you my mother?"

When Ms. Schultz said yes, "I just fell into her arms. It felt so natural," Ms. Harris said. "We held on for the longest time."

Ms. Harris, who is married and has a daughter of her own, said her adoptive parents supported her decision to find her birth parents. She said she was sixteen when she first thought about starting the search, but waited until she felt she was old enough to cope with what she might find.

Mother and daughter had lived only two streets apart for the past two years.

The pair plan to search together for Ms. Harris's brothers, Tim and Terry.

Israeli Wakes to Masked Nurses Thought To Be from Heaven, Hell

TEL AVIV (Reuters) — An Israeli hospital patient, roused by a missile alert after two weeks of sedation, thought he was in heaven or hell when he awoke surrounded by doctors in gas masks.

The Beilinson Medical Center intensive care director said that the forty-two-year-old man was sedated after kidney and pancreas transplant operations.

"When he woke up he saw these strange-looking people around him. He didn't realize, of course, he was in the middle of an air raid," the director told Reuters.

The surgeon removed his mask and tried to reassure the patient, passing on the best regards of what he thought was the man's mother.

"But unfortunately his real mother [had] passed away four years ago," the director said. The surgeon's regards were actually from another woman visiting the hospital with the patient's father.

"So now it was crystal clear to the patient that he had died," the director said.

Twin Sisters' Cars Collide

ELMWOOD, WIS. (AP) — A woman was in fair condition with head injuries after her car collided with her identical twin sister's at an intersection, authorities said.

Jean Bechel, nineteen, was hospitalized in Eau Claire after the accident near here, officials said. Jan Bechel, who lives with her sister and their parents in Plum City, suffered minor injuries.

Register Children as Sheep, Conference Told

DUNEDIN, NEW ZEALAND (AP) — Registering children as sheep is one way New Zealand families might be able to afford to bring up children, an economist told a conference.

As sheep, their food, accommodation, and other expenses would be tax deductible, Brian Easton told the conference on childrearing. "The mother might even be eligible for shepherd's wages," he said.

Easton said parents in New Zealand are required to make great sacrifices to raise children, and their financial struggles are largely ignored.

New Zealand, dependent on a rural economy, has some 60 million sheep and 3.3 million people.

Sister Imitating Sister Electrocutes Self

BANGKOK (Reuters) — A woman showing neighbors how her sister electrocuted herself later also electrocuted herself, a Thai newspaper reported.

Yooket Paen, fifty-seven, of Angthong, a rural area 100 km (60 miles) north of Bangkok, slipped in farmyard mud, grabbed a live wire, and died, the Thai-language *Daily News* reported.

Her sister, Yooket Pan, fifty-two, showed neighbors later in the day how the accident happened. She slipped, grabbed the live wire, and died.

A Race to the Finish

Meet Jatti, the Most Beautiful Sheep in Pakistan

ISLAMABAD (Reuters) — Jatti the ewe has been crowned the most beautiful sheep in Pakistan for 1991.

The fluffy charmer from Dhakoo village in Chakwal district celebrated her victory by dancing to traditional Pakistani music, the PPI news agency reported.

"She also greeted and pleased the audience by putting her front leg to her forehead as a gesture of Salaam [greeting] to the overjoyed crowd," the agency said.

Jatti beat out an estimated two thousand other contenders in the sheep beauty contest.

Last year's winner, Sohni, was not even a runner-up.

"Due to giving birth to several offspring, she has lost her charms and beauty," the agency said.

DJ Asks for Eggs, Postmaster Gets the Yolk

BALA CYNWYD, PA. (UPI) — Breakfast came with the mail Tuesday at radio station WEGX-FM, but the eggs were a trifle runny.

Gooey envelopes started arriving at the station after morning disk jockey John Lander offered $1,000 to the first listener who could get an unbroken raw egg through the mail.

One man succeeded. Hundreds failed. The result was not a pretty sight. "We had a lot of messy mail," said Bala Cynwyd Postmaster Mark Glenn. "But it's our job to deliver it."

Glenn said people began dropping off eggs at the post office Monday morning, hours after Lander announced the contest. Most had been stuffed into ordinary envelopes.

Glenn smelled something rotten, but he was duty bound to deliver the mail. By early Tuesday morning, more than one hundred lumpy envelopes had accumulated in the sorting bins.

"We postmarked them and put them into a plastic container," he said. "Then we dropped them all off at the station. A lot of them didn't make it."

The folks at WEGX-FM said they didn't mind the

mess. "It was a lot of fun," said David Noll, who runs the station.

Noll said a postmarked envelope containing an intact raw egg arrived at the station late Monday afternoon. He said the sender, an Upper Darby man, is the apparent winner of the contest.

"He mailed it at the main post office in Philadelphia," Noll said. "It came in a regular number ten envelope with a legal postmark. I don't know how it got through in one piece. We're checking it out."

Polish By-Election Draws Turnout of One

WARSAW (Reuters) — A candidate in a local Polish by-election voted courteously for his opponent and lost the seat. He was the only person to vote.

The Official PAP news agency did not name the candidate, the only one of the 595 voters in Mragowo, in northeastern Poland, who bothered to cast a ballot.

Mayor's Candidate Is Disqualified

SAN ANTERO, COLOMBIA (UPI) — Mayor Jorge Morales is sad and is disconsolately seeking another candidate to compete with dignity in an unusual contest taking place in San Antero.

Each year, with the support of the San Antero municipality, 550 km north of Bogota, a contest is organized for the prettiest donkey, the donkeys being the everyday work animals for peasants.

Morales entered "La Sampa" as his candidate, but the veterinarians designated by the judge to physically examine the contenders for the title discovered that the mayor's entry had lost her virginity and she was immediately disqualified.

From now on, each donkey candidate will be an honorary citizen of San Antero and will receive from the mayor's hands the Gold Donkey Bag.

Court Affirms Election Victory of Dead Judge

OKLAHOMA CITY (AP) — The Oklahoma Supreme Court upheld the landslide election of a dead judge against a living candidate, saying the results must be interpreted as a vote against the loser.

Incumbent Frank M. Ogden III, who died August 11, won 91 percent of the vote cast November 6 in a race against Josh L. Evans, who had challenged the results.

"It is beyond question that the will of the elector-

ate was to cast votes for Judge Ogden and against candidate Evans," the Supreme Court said Tuesday.

The result leaves the job open for an appointment by the governor.

Bovine Bingo

SPRING LAKE, MICH. (AP) — Business leaders are betting on Bovine Bingo to bring in the big bucks.

The game of chance involves players guessing where a well-fed cow will leave its droppings on a lawn-sized bingo card. Players purchase a square on a marked field, and the winner is the one whose square is chosen by the cow.

"It's a unique way to raise money," said Eric DeLong, the manager of Spring Lake, a village a few miles inland from Lake Michigan's west-central coast.

Bovine bingo is the successor to rubber-duck

races and donkey basketball, two other games sponsored by the Spring Lake Central Business District Development Authority to raise money to promote the village.

The cow will make its debut during this June's Spring Lake Heritage Festival.

Business leaders are auditioning cows for the part.

"We believe finding a cow volunteer is probably the easiest part of the whole project," DeLong said.

Odor-Eaters Contest

MONTPELIER, VT. (AP) — Ah! Spring! Bees are buzzing, birds are singing, flowers are blooming.

In Montpelier, however, spring is accompanied by an unmistakable sound and odor: a squish and squeal of lost soles, grisly grommets, gnawed Nikes, and reeking Reeboks known as the Sixteenth Annual Odor-Eaters International Rotten Sneaker Contest.

Each year, on the first day of spring, kids from across the country converge on this otherwise peaceful and pleasant-smelling town to decide who truly has achieved the agony of de-feet and with it a place in the airtight Hall of Fumes.

While kids from ages five to eighteen go tongue-to-toe for the dubious honor of having owned the worst sneakers on the planet, the mothers of these champions give a sigh of relief as the noxious sneakers leave home forever, their fragrance never to be inhaled again.

More than anyone else, mothers understand just how rotten a sneaker can be. "Being a mother has really prepared me for judging this year's collection of tattered tennies," says Ann Cumming, mayor of Montpelier and mother. Mayor Cumming is a seasoned veteran of rotten sneaker contests who feels that her years of braving dark, dank closets have prepared her well.

"I really think that it's the mothers who are the unsung heroes of this contest," adds Dr. Herbert Lapidus, the head judge, chief odorologist, and the inventor of Odor-Eaters. "Having nosed my way through many of these contests, I have a great respect for the strength and valor of the mothers of our winners. My standards for a true winner are based on the twenty-foot formula.*

Contenders for the title must prove that their sneakers are truly rotten and can stay on their feet

* The 20-foot formula is that Dr. Lapidus can detect a run-nerup at ten feet, a sure-fire champion at fifteen feet, and the international winner at twenty feet or more. When Dr. Lapidus first judged the contest, in 1988, he had a five-foot rule. Since then, the aroma of fetid footwear has become pronouncedly worse.

during the contest. "We can spot an impostor in the blink of an eye and a whiff of the schnoz," says Dr. Lapidus.

Man Who Advertised for Love on His Van Hits the Jackpot

CUBA, N.Y. (AP) — A man met the woman of his dreams by advertising on the side of his van and said it was like winning a "lottery for women."

John Koehler, fifty-two, was swamped with telephone calls and letters after he was written up in newspapers for an unusual dating ploy. He bannered his van with a sign that said, "WANTED—Female 35 to 45, must like children, camping, quiet times, pets. Hardworking man; lots of attention. Call. It doesn't hurt to talk."

"The phone started ringing at four P.M. that afternoon and didn't stop for months," said Koehler, who lives in the Rochester suburb of Spencerport.

"I felt like I had won the New York State lottery for women."

But the only query that mattered was a letter from the village of Cuba, seventy-five miles southwest of Rochester, where Bobbi Zirbel's mother had urged her to write.

"After all the other women he met, I'm surprised he picked me," said Zirbel, thirty-three.

The couple has been dating since last April and plans to get married in a year or so.

What most impressed Koehler, a painter and wallpaper hanger, was the content of Zirbel's letter. "She didn't write about herself and her needs and wants," he said. "She told me about her dog and her plants and wrote a paragraph about each of her kids."

Ain't You Got No Culture?

Union Leaders Seek to Fight Antistrike Erotic Films

SÃO PAULO, BRAZIL (Reuters) — The management at a mining company here has a new approach to strikebreaking: show the employees erotic films.

According to union leaders, company officials at Companhia Vale do Rio Doce have been playing erotic films to entice nonstriking workers to stay in the factory.

Union leaders are meeting in Rio de Janeiro to consider how to confront the new management tactic, the newsweekly *Veja* reported.

Veja said that union leaders are considering showing the same films to the strikers.

Japanese Firm Makes Musical Bra in Fitting Mozart Tribute

TOKYO (Reuters) — A Japanese lingerie firm seeking a fitting way to mark Mozart's bicentenary year has come up with a musical bra.

The bra, in indigo blue with musical staff motif repeated on matching panties, is studded with tiny lights that flash when the music plays, a spokeswoman for Triumph International Japan said.

There is one drawback, however.

"Since it involves electronic devices, it's no good for regular use," the spokeswoman said. "It can't be washed."

Musical Weirdos

WASHINGTON, D.C. (AP) — Want to stand out from the musical crowd? Try playing the Jingling Johnny. Become a virtuoso on the oliphant. Or tootle on the world's largest ocarina.

These oddities are found in the Smithsonian Institution's collection of more than three thousand musical instruments, which range alphabetically from accordions to zithers, with a lot of strange stuff in between.

Sharing space with Stradivari's revered 1701 Servais cello and Paderewski's Steinway grand is the Jingling Johnny, a brass contraption of tiny bells, umbrellas, and scimitars hung from a pole that was shaken by Turkish marching bands to make a merry tinkling sound.

There are banjos fashioned from pie plates and sifters covered with groundhog skin. Another was carved from wood by a southern plantation slave. A U.S. infantryman idling in France after World War I made his banjo from a German artillery shell with machine-gun shells for tuning pegs.

The array of harmonicas, 654 at last count, includes a novelty item called the mouth organ, which can genteelly be described only as X-rated.

Collection manager Gary Sturm said the rarest instrument in the collection is a lavishly decorated, double-manual Stehlin harpsichord made in pre-Revolutionary France in 1770. It's one of only three by its maker known to exist.

One of the most obscure instruments is a xylophone from Chile that consists of a row of petrified rocks.

Sturm said the biggest gap in the Smithsonian collection, which is open only to serious musical scholars, is instruments from the rock 'n' roll era. "We don't have any electric guitars, not even one of

Leo Fender's Stratocasters," he said. "The twentieth century is nearly over, and we've got to get on it."

Oh, about the world's largest ocarina.

This contrabass wind instrument is dark green and looks like a watermelon. It was custom made in the 1940s for a dance band musician who was tired of lugging his string bass from gig to gig.

"The ocarina arrived one day on a Greyhound bus from Florida, with a letter saying the owner was giving it to the Smithsonian," Sturm said.

"We figured it would cost us twenty dollars to send it back, so we kept it."

Chinese Takeout Now an Object of Art

NEW YORK (AP) — Choose from column A. Enjoy anything from column B. But with two, you don't get an egg roll.

Chopsticks, fortune cookies, and cardboard containers—the various trappings of Chinese takeout—are all the rage at a downtown Manhattan gallery.

The walls of the Franklin Furnace Museum are plastered with five thousand menus. Restaurant shopping bags hang from the ceiling. A life-size delivery-man doll perches on a bicycle in the window.

The exhibit, called "A Million Menus," is described as a celebration of Chinese takeout food in America. It was put together by Harley Spiller, the museum's administrative director and self-described "obsessive collector."

Spiller combined the unusual with the mundane. A 1916 menu of the Oriental Restaurant in Chinatown shows an early example of takeout. "We put up orders so that they may be taken home," it reads.

The Peking Duck House supplied a menu autographed by a loyal patron, former Mayor Edward I. Koch.

There's a copy of a letter that then Vice President Richard Nixon sent to the Chinese American Restaurant Association in 1958 congratulating the organization on its twenty-sixth anniversary.

And there's the fortune cookie. An entire glass case is devoted to them, which Spiller says are as Chinese as chicken chow mein. His favorite fortune: "He loves you as much as he can, but he cannot love you very much."

Visitors can peruse scores of business cards and calendars from Chinese restaurants, or enter a fortune-writing contest.

A bag of Crispy Chinese TV Snacks is attached to

a television that plays a videotape of delivery men at work.

The exhibit has drawn thousands since it opened Feb. 15 on the Chinese New Year, Spiller said. Schoolchildren squeal in delight at the eight-foot-long chopsticks that Spiller's father carved for the show, and sometimes pedestrians wander in thinking the museum is a Chinese restaurant.

Spiller said he began gathering Chinese menus ten years ago when he moved to Manhattan after growing up in Buffalo and attending Northwestern University in Evanston, Ill.

Spiller, an English major, said he started collecting the menus because he liked looking for mistakes in grammar. The hobby soon turned into an obsession.

"It was out there, free, and I took it in," he said.

"When I grew up, Chinese food was a treat on Sunday night. In New York it was everywhere."

After receiving a grant for the show about two years ago, Spiller widened his search. He enlisted the help of friends and family, contacted chambers of commerce, and mailed out requests for menus and other items to restaurants around the country.

Spiller said one purpose of the show is to make clear that Chinese takeout food is a U.S. phenomenon. "There's a lot more to Chinese culture than food," he said.

Strippers Hold Reunion at Museum of Au Naturel *History*

HELENDALE, CALIF. (AP) — The Smithsonian may have Archie Bunker's chair, but the Strippers Hall of Fame displays the silver-sequined pasties worn by Jennie "The Bazoom Girl" Lee.

It also boasts Jayne Mansfield's sofa—pink, of

course—and Blaze Starr's autographed photo: nude, of course.

They're all on display at a museum operated by sixty-five-year-old Dixie Evans, a self-described Marilyn Monroe of burlesque.

One weekend strippers past and present who belong to the five hundred-strong Exotic Dancers League of America arrived in Helendale, well off the beaten path in the Mojave Desert eighty miles northeast of Los Angeles, to talk shop and drop tops.

The gathering attracted names that used to drive men wild: Dusty Sage, Sheri Champagne, Jeanine "Eye-Full Tower" France, Flame O'Neil, and Tanayo, the "Costa Rican Dream Girl."

Some of them are grandmothers now, but they squeezed into sleeveless gold lamé dresses and skimpy pink bras.

Over fried chicken and macaroni salad the strippers talked about the good old days, when stripping was more show business than just show and the final flash of flesh came only after an excruciatingly long bump-and-grind buildup.

Some of them put on a brief show Friday on a stage at the end of a pool behind the museum, strutting to a tape recording of "The Stripper."

Though the kicks weren't as elastic and the flesh shook a bit more than it used to, they ended the production to hearty applause and a few whistles.

Trashy Art

ALEXANDRIA, VA. (AP) — The National Endowment for the Arts and its critics may bicker over what's good art and what's not, but everybody strolling through a local gallery's new exhibition agrees that the works on display are pure trash.

Fancy a full-length woman's coat knitted from plastic garbage bags? It's yours for a mere three thousand dollars. If that's too steep, there's a rustic, hand-painted little table mounted on the truck of an old Christmas tree for fifteen hundred dollars.

Selling for $250 is the ultimate in trash art—nearly three hundred throwaway items that have been compacted by artist Katherine Cantwell of Chicago into an eighteen-inch ball held together with wheat paste. She says the goodies inside include an Arby's restaurant place mat, a Spiegel mail-order catalog, candy, tea bag and Band-Aid wrappers, a Tampax instruction sheet, airline luggage tags, paycheck stubs, calendar pages, and a Dunkin' Donuts bag.

"This show proves that you can make art out of almost anything," said metalsmith Eric Margry, who conceived of this exhibition given at the Torpedo Factory Art Center, an artists' cooperative in this Washington suburb.

The twenty-eight artists represented in the show, which is titled Second Chance, rummaged through

attics, garages, and old drawers for useless, long-forgotten objects that could be reincarnated as artistic creations.

Artist Carol Buchman, of Cambridge, Mass., won a juror's trophy for her "Art City," a scale-model metropolis fashioned from cereal boxes, radio tubes, fishing bobs, canapé toothpicks, and other junk scavenged from her home.

Awards also went to Jill Kimball of New York for a fanciful work with a metal drain cover, and to Fabian Kuttner, of Charlottesville, Va., for his chair made from an old water heater.

Quentin M. Davis, of State College, Pa., won a trophy for his piece *Book for the Dead*, which was fabricated from roadside debris.

Chained and bound in the rubber tread from a discarded truck tire, this book's pages of recycled refuse contain photocopied images of dead squirrels and graffiti scrawled by viewers, who are invited to philosophize about death.

The show also includes a model biplane made from Schlitz beer cans, a functioning coffeemaker fashioned from scraps of old coffee cans, a floor lamp made from a bowling ball and tenpin, and sculptures made from rusted picture frames, stovepipes, clock parts, saw blades, a truck panel, and sardine cans.

"A lot of people come in here and ask, 'Is this the junk show?' or 'Is this the trash show?'" said art center administrator Mary Evans. "I have trouble with that. These works represent the same amount of work and imagination and creative effort that you find in some museums."

Dogs Barred from Dog Museum

St. Louis (AP) — Dogs are no longer welcome on the carpet at the Dog Museum.

The reason: too many canine accidents and too many fleas.

It used to be that dogs on leashes could browse through galleries full of paintings, sculptures and photographs of dogs.

But then, "You'd walk into a gallery and you'd see a big wet spot there, and you'd say, uh, great," said Gail Haynes, the museum's business manager.

Not only that, but fleas left behind by shaggy visitors were biting the ankles of museum workers.

Dogs and their masters can still visit the community room. That's where the videotapes on dog breeds and dog training are stored.

That's also the room with the tile floor.

Chew and Spit

WASHINGTON-ON-THE-BRAZOS, TEX. (AP) — European visitors found it repulsive. Texans, on the other hand, loved it. Sam Houston is said to have been addicted to it.

And now the operators of the Star of the Republic Museum here want people to remember how pervasive the practice of tobacco chewing and spitting was in the early days of Texas.

"That's what's pretty exciting about working here. You can deal with all aspects of life," Sherry Humphreys, curator of exhibits at the museum, says of her exhibit entitled "Chew, Chew, Chew and Spit, Spit, Spit: Tobacco in the Texas Republic."

"You're not limited to major military events or the political events, even though they're terribly important. Everybody knows that and we don't try to downplay that at all, but these are just things that people don't normally think about."

The chew-and-spit presentation includes displays of advertisements for things like spittoons, an example of roped tobacco, pictures, explanations, and an authentic snuffbox of the era.

The exhibit's title is drawn from a letter written by a British traveler, Francis Sheridan, from Galveston in 1842.

"High and low, rich and poor, young and old, chew, chew, chew and spit, spit, spit, all the blessed day and most of the night," Sheridan wrote, complaining about the "incessant remorseless spitting" of tobacco juice and use of other tobacco products.

Sheridan wrote that he once watched a man teaching his two-year-old son in Galveston how to spit "and loudly applauding every successful effort of the precious prodigy."

"No gentleman would think of smoking in a parlor with ladies present without first asking their permission, yet he would not hesitate to chew, and its necessary sequel, to spit," Ms. Humphreys said. Tobacco's critics have, however, blamed it for "perverted sexuality, impotency and cancer."

In keeping with the museum's interests regard-

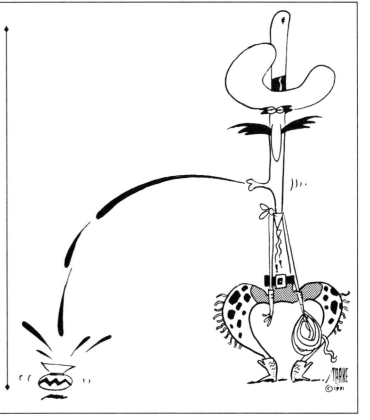

ing everyday life, the tobacco exhibit shares a hallway with a presentation about Texas bathrooms entitled "Johnnies and Epicurean Innovations."

It includes comments from an obviously more genteel visitor to early Texas who noted that although Texans washed their hands and faces daily, both men and women were more inclined to wash their bodies from year to year.

"Texans have great natural facilities for bathing," a visitor named Edward Smith once wrote. "But we scarcely found a Texan who took advantage of them. As a general rule, they were not wasteful of soap and water."

That's My Mummy: Church and State Fight for Their Knight

NEUSTADT, GERMANY (AP)—Once a powerful knight clad in iron mail, Sir Friedrich von Kahlbutz now spends his days gazing vacantly from a glass-covered coffin rigged with burglar alarms.

He is a true scientific wonder, a puzzle that experts have studied but can't fully explain. While others decayed, Kahlbutz became a naturally occurring mummy—a bit thin, perhaps, but perfectly intact.

Kahlbutz fathered forty-one children while he was alive but has proved even more popular in death, annually drawing tens of thousands of tourists to see the shriveled nobleman from a feudal era.

But now Kahlbutz has become a prize in a very modern jousting match that has pitted church against state in this tiny east German town.

The mayor and the local pastor both claim ownership of the money-making mummy. At stake is enough tourist dollars to renovate a church or build a municipal parking lot.

Much mystery and legend, enhanced by the locals, surrounds the mummy. "We have to clip his fingernails every week," contends a dead-serious Hildegard Mathiske, the caretaker.

One legend says the knight killed a shepherd who refused to subject his wife to the knight's ravishments. Kahlbutz supposedly denied the killing.

"If I am responsible, let my body never decay," he supposedly said.

Mad Menagerie

Naughty Dog

GRAPEVINE, TEX. (AP) — Nationally known obedience trainer Terri Arnold may want to work on the command *stay*.

Her golden retriever wandered away from its airline carrier at Dallas–Fort Worth International Airport. When the plane's doors opened, the dog plain took off.

Was it Naughty? Of course. Naughty is the dog's name.

But freedom turned out to be for the dogs. Naughty was spotted doing things like wandering in front of taxiing airplanes.

Delta Airlines, dog lovers, and dog-retrieval specialists teamed up to find it.

So the story does have a happy ending: Arnold retrieved the retriever.

Giraffe Barbecue

JOHANNESBURG, SOUTH AFRICA (AP) — Plans for what is believed to be the world's first giraffe barbecue have drawn protests from animal-rights groups, according to one report.

The *Star* newspaper said a social group called Die Afrikaner Klub plants to roast a 2,800-pound giraffe on a six-yard-long spit. It said it would take twenty hours to cook the animal.

The newspaper said the event appeared to be the world's first giraffe barbecue.

Charles Harper, the chairman of the club, said there was strong interest in the event and that the club had already sold three hundred tickets at forty dollars each.

Barbecues, called *braais* in South Africa, are a popular form of entertainment there.

Several animal-rights groups denounced the plan.

They said it was irresponsible to kill a wild animal as a "gimmick."

"It is extremely barbaric to stick a giraffe on a spit. Surely we are trying to move away from this type of thing. It totally devalues wildlife," said Christine Berry of Beauty Without Cruelty.

But a spokeswoman for the Society for the Prevention of Cruelty to Animals said the barbecue was not illegal, since giraffes are not on the endangered animal list. The society said it was no worse than slaughtering a cow or a sheep.

One Man's Answer to the Rat Explosion: Contraceptives

KESALAHTI, FINLAND (AP) — Rats aren't much of a problem in clean, cold Finland, and Kalle Heiskanen hopes to keep it that way. So he feeds them contraceptives.

He said he has come to like the rats and doesn't want them wiped out, just kept to manageable numbers.

Have people laughed at Heiskanen? "Sure. I was labeled Rat Professor, Hormone Heiskanen . . . the village clown."

But, he added, "playing the flute would only mean taking the problem elsewhere," a sly reference to a piper who solved a rat problem in Hamelin, Germany, several centuries ago.

People have also taken Heiskanen seriously. Scientists at the local university suggested progesterone, a hormone that resembles substances used in contraceptive pills. University pharmacists provided Heiskanen with a mixture of progesterone and cooking oil, with advice on how to feed and observe rats.

The Kesalahti Council gave him a five hundred

dollar grant, which let him go to the garbage dump on the edge of Kesalahti, ten miles from the Soviet border.

He lived there in a trailer for two months, feeding six hundred to seven hundred rats every night with bread soaked in the progesterone mixture. When he continued his nighttime patrols afterward, he said the rat population had shrunk about 15 percent in four months.

Farmer of Exotic Animals Warms to Task of Hatching Emu Chicks

MARION, N.Y. (AP) — When an ice storm knocked out the power at a woman's home and exotic animal farm, she made herself into a human incubator and spent three days lying on a couch with fifteen live eggs stuffed in her clothes.

Claire Luteyn and her husband, Donald, devised the plan to save fifteen emu eggs they hoped would hatch into emu chicks, which are worth $1,000 to $1,500 each. Emus are Australian relatives of the ostrich.

Fifteen of the forest-green eggs were in the Luteyns' incubator when a March storm knocked out the power to their home and more then three hundred thousand others.

The emu eggs, which require a temperature of 97 degrees and a humidity of 84 percent, seemed doomed, but the Luteyns improvised quickly.

Luteyn dressed in a nightgown, put the eggs on her chest and stomach, then put on a warm jumpsuit to cover them. She spent three days on the couch, seldom straying from her roost.

The baseball-size eggs weighed about one and a half pounds each and had to be turned every two and a half hours.

So far nine of the fifteen eggs have hatched. Luteyn said she will know within two weeks whether the other six will also. The chicks will be sold when they are about five weeks old.

The Luteyns have raised exotic birds and animals at their western New York farm for about five years. Their collection includes four adult emus, llamas, miniature donkeys, and a miniature dachshund.

Stranded Elephants

MADISON, PA. (AP) — An animal keeper and five elephants who had truck trouble on the way to the circus are leaving a gift that will make sure a mechanic will never forget the visitors he sheltered.

The elephants, owned by the Hawthorne Co. of Chicago, were headed from Harrisburg to a Shriner's Circus in Detroit when their truck had engine trouble on I-70.

They arrived Monday evening at Dave's Welding and Heavy Equipment Repair in Madison. There Ritenour provided water, electricity, and space for the elephants.

Garage owner Dave Ritenour, who is also a farmer, said his fruit trees will benefit from the manure the elephants leave.

"All together, they produce a couple hundred pounds of manure every day," handler Ed South said. "It's some of the best fertilizer in the world."

"Next year, we'll have peaches this big," said Ritenour, gesturing as a fisherman would to describe his catch.

"It's just another stop in the road for them," South said. "All they care about is that they've got food and water. As long as they've got that, they're pretty contented."

Ritenour said he expected to have South's truck fixed sometime Friday.

Chinese Hens Looking Through Rose-colored Glasses May Lay More

BEIJING (Reuters) — China has put rose-colored contact lenses on 140 hens to test whether they will produce more eggs, the official source *Farmers Daily* said.

The newspaper said that red lenses may calm the chickens, increase production, and "effectively correct the chickens' bad habit of pecking their anuses."

Gao Jinyuan, manager of the chicken test farm in the coastal city of Hangzhou, said the experiment, which uses U.S. technology, could increase egg production by 6 percent.

Chilled Milk?
Dairy Farmers Try to
Keep Cows from
Udderly Freezing

COLUMBIA, MO. (AP) — To beat a lack of heat, some dairy farmers are using cow brassieres and hair dryers to keep their animals from udderly freezing.

"You've got to try to keep a cold cow comfortable, or you're going to lose a lot of milk production," said Barry Stevens, a University of Missouri dairy specialist.

Some farmers use nylon-mesh udder supports on animals that calved recently and have their udders swollen with milk, he said. Others use hair dryers and towels to keep moisture off the animals.

Mean Moose

JACKSON, WYO. (AP) — A 1,200-pound pregnant moose occupied a barn for several days, repeatedly charging the landowner and shaking off tranquilizer darts before deciding to move on.

Landowner John Forester even carried a gun to escort his children to the bus stop.

"She was one Mean Mildred," said Wyoming Game and Fish officer Tom Tillman.

The moose appeared one weekend, plump with calf, on Forester's property near Grand Teton National Park in northwestern Wyoming. "She was just looking for a place to rest, and the barn was perfect," Forester said. "It provided shelter, had water, and there was hay for the horses."

But when Forester tried to get into the barn to feed his horses, Mean Mildred charged. To try to scare her away, he fired two rounds from a gun into the air.

"She turned right around and turned her ears flat and came right at me," he said.

He dodged into some nearby bushes. Then he called the Game and Fish agency, and Tillman arrived with a gun that shoots whistling firecrackers. The moose wouldn't budge.

"I chased her around for a while, then she chased me around for a while. She was pretty aggressive," Tillman said.

On Tuesday morning Tillman returned with a tranquilizer gun, but that appeared to have no effect. While he was trying another tactic the moose suddenly leaped up, bolted over the fence, and ran away.

She has since been seen about two hundred yards from the house, but has not returned to terrorize the family. "Lots of people have confrontations with moose around here, but only one in a thousand moose respond the way she did," Tillman said.

Dog Rescued After Dangling for Nine Days

Oslo (AP) — A dog named Bonzo leaped a farm fence but caught his foot and dangled upside down for nine days, living on snow while awaiting rescue, a newspaper reported.

"I had given up hope," Bonzo's owner, Torstein Nerbraaten, told the newspaper *Dagbladet* after the border collie was rescued near Nor-Aurdal, in midwestern Norway.

The forty-nine-year-old farmer said he had searched for and advertised in the local newspaper in hopes of finding Bonzo.

Alerted by a soft whine, a passerby discovered the seven-year-old dog in a thicket near the farm last week, hanging upside down with his head in the snow.

"I was unbelievably happy," Nerbraaten said. But no happier than thin, limping Bonzo.

"When I managed to free him, he immediately licked me all over. I have never in my life seen such a happy dog," he said.

Australian Police Attacked with Frozen Kangaroo Tails

Sydney (Reuters) — Australian police patrolling an outback highway were attacked Friday by a group of aborigines wielding frozen kangaroo tails.

The two officers were set upon by about fifteen aborigines with yard-long frozen kangaroo tails when they tried to remove another aborigine who was sitting in the middle of the Stuart Highway trying to commit suicide, a police sergeant said.

"It sounds humorous, but it was quite frightening.

The officers suffered bruises and cuts, but nothing serious," Sgt. Phil Clapin said by telephone from Alice Springs.

Clapin said the attack occurred near the small outback town of Tea Tree, about 120 miles north of Alice Springs.

He said frozen kangaroo tails were shipped into the outback from Adelaide, primarily for aboriginal consumption. "It saves them going out and killing the kangaroos themselves," he said.

Trainer Teaches Asian Elephant to Paint

ANCHORAGE, ALA. (AP) — She's no Jackson Pollock, and her work may not be ready for the Museum of Modern Art. But she has joined one select group of artists: painting pachyderms.

Annabelle the Asian elephant took up painting early this year and completed her first solo effort February 19. Her work is hanging in the Anchorage Zoo coffee shop.

Will Soho be next?

She is only a novice, of course, but her trainer, David Hall, is convinced Annabelle is a four-ton bundle of talent. "I think it's good, but I'm prejudiced," he said. "I think it honestly equals any of the abstract art I've seen, but I never understood that anyway."

Annabelle's work has impressed so many people at the zoo that her works will be displayed at a show at the end of June, Hall said. And he added that he expects several of her works to sell.

Soho may be next.

Hall is Annabelle's only art critic at the moment. He says that she probably does not paint as well as one elephant at the San Diego Zoo. So far he has kept seven works, including a favorite that has what looks like a black arrow on the paper.

"I don't know how she did it," he said

To demonstrate her technique, Annabelle had a painting session one afternoon. Hall loaded a brush with blue acrylic paint and handed it to the eight thousand-pound artist. Grasping the brush with the end of her flexible trunk, Annabelle began making vertical strokes on the paper.

She missed the mark about half the time and hit the mounting board. Hall had to reload the brush every few strokes because, as might be expected, Annabelle has a heavy trunk.

"She has improved 100 percent in the last month," he said while coaxing her to make her mark. "She's a lot freer with her paint strokes."

One who did not appear impressed with Annabelle's artistic abilities was Maggie, the smaller, African elephant who shares her quarters at the zoo. While Annabelle painted, Maggie looked the other way and ate hay.

Animal Court Judge Hears Beastly Disputes

VENTURA, CALIF. (AP) — The feathers can fly and litigants sometimes engage in swinish behavior in Kathy Jenks's courtroom.

She's Ventura County's poundmaster and runs the creature court. Once a month she holds hearings in the basement of the county administration building to settle complaints about pets. She has heard nearly four hundred cases in four years.

Animals of the nonhuman kind aren't allowed in, though in one case Jenks recalls that involved a dog owner, you might not have known from the sound of it.

"During the hearing, the man declared that he was no longer a member of the human race and was now a dog," Jenks said. "He barked for the next hour."

Faithful Sheepdog

METZ, FRANCE (AFP) — Rex, a seven-year-old Belgian sheepdog, walked more than 1,000 km (600 miles) home from Nimes, in southern France, to find his master at Ban-Saint-Martin near here.

"It's a miracle. I just don't know how he did it," Rex's owner René Schoenedecker said of the dog's seven-month journey.

On September 18, Rex ran away from Mr. Schoenedecker's nephew, who had taken him down to the south for training.

He at last turned up, exhausted, on his master's doorstep—to find that Mr. Schoenedecker had moved. The dog was finally reunited with his master after his son phoned to tell him the extraordinary news.

I Couldn't Help Myself

Luggage Lover

LOS ANGELES (AP) — Most people buy luggage so they can leave home. One man buys his luggage to take home.

"People are really funny when they come into my apartment," said St. Jivago Desanges. "After they get over the shock, the first thing they usually ask is if I'm moving."

The travel buff has stacked his one-bedroom apartment with one hundred pieces of luggage, a dozen boxes with maps and travel brochures, one thousand hotel room keys, and thirty thousand vintage hotel stickers.

"I guess it is kind of strange," he said. "I don't know many homes that have trunks staring you in the face when you walk in the door."

"There are a lot of reasons for collecting luggage," said the hobbyist, who says his passion is shared by Tom Selleck, Jerry Lewis, Donna Summer, and Heather Locklear. "Obviously, there's the practical side. They do keep things organized. But I have always been fascinated by the craftsmanship involved in luggage. And, of course, there's always the nostalgia involved with travel."

When Desanges is not trying to outbid other luggage lovers for the former cases of Henry and Clare Booth Luce or actor Joseph Cotten, he travels five months a year with his favorite suitcase, a Louis Vuitton train case.

The forty-four-year-old photographer's collection has its uses. Stacked ceiling high in his living room, dining room, and bedroom, the cases store his clothes. But he says there are drawbacks: "It takes a little time getting dressed in the morning."

Glass Vandal

LOS ANGELES (AP) — A thrill-seeking glass salesman who roamed the San Fernando Valley shooting out storefront windows was placed on probation.

Richard Angona, thirty-nine, was also ordered to perform community service and pay fifteen thousand dollars in restitution to store owners.

He pleaded guilty to felony vandalism for shooting out thirty-two windows with a BB gun over five months. Angona received three years' probation.

Under the terms of a plea bargain, Superior Court Judge Michael Farrell dismissed four other felony vandalism charges. Each count carried a maximum of one year in prison and a ten thousand dollar fine.

Authorities initially suspected that Angona had shot out the windows in an attempt to drum up business for a North Hollywood glass company where he worked, Deputy District Attorney James Baker said.

But it was later determined "to be more for the thrill of seeing glass shatter and break," the prosecutor said, adding that it was Angona's way to relieve stress. "He admitted it was fun to watch the glass fall."

"Toe Licker" Strikes on San Francisco College Campus

SAN FRANCISCO (Reuters) — Female students at San Francisco State University want to put a stop to the man they call the "toe licker."

A young man described by his victims as a "normal-looking guy" has been sneaking into the dormitory rooms of women at night, lifting their blankets, and licking their toes and legs.

The latest incident took place one weekend, and two others occurred last September, the San Francisco *Chronicle* reported.

"What is it with this licking thing, anyway?"

student Rhonelle DeLeon, twenty, told the newspaper. "It's pretty bizarre."

All the attacks took place at the same dormitory but involved three different women. In each case the man escaped and no injuries were reported.

Female students said they were taking extra care in locking their doors at night and keeping baseball bats and other potential weapons at their bedsides.

Man with Faucet Obsession after Accident Gets Damages

HONG KONG (Reuters) — Hong Kong watchman Lee Wun has had an uncontrollable urge to turn on faucets since he was hit by a truck and suffered brain damage.

The High Court awarded sixty-nine-year-old Lee $116,666 in damages against the driver, saying part of the award was to cover the increased water bills resulting from his obsession.

Swiss Chomp Their Way to New Chocolate Record

BERNE, SWITZERLAND (Reuters) — The Swiss staunchly defended their record as the world's biggest chocolate eaters last year, consuming a record 11.3 kg (25 pounds) per head, the trade association Choco-suisse says.

The Swiss produced 108.9 tons of chocolate worth 910 million dollars in 1990—and ate two-thirds of it themselves.

German Police Hunt Fancy Shoe Thief

KASSEL, GERMANY (Reuters) — Police in Kassel are hot on the heels of a thief who ambushes women and makes off with their fancy shoes.

The man has attacked twelve women, aged between twenty and forty, in this small central German city. Some needed treatment for shock, but most reacted calmly.

"He tackles women walking alone at night, pulls their shoes off, and escapes into the darkness," said Gerhard Dippmann, a Kassel detective. "He is only interested in their shoes. The women have not been injured and no money has been stolen."

Car 54, Where Are You?

Ill-fitting Underwear Helps Australian Escape Prison Term

NEW DELHI (AP) — A young Australian sentenced to ten years in prison for carrying hashish in his underwear was acquitted by a court when he proved that the underwear produced in evidence did not fit him.

Andrews Salvador had been given a ten-year term plus a fine of about $27,700 by a lower court after his arrest, Press Trust of India reported. It said he had been arrested just before boarding a flight from Thiruvananthapuram, in the southern Indian state of Kerala, to Bombay, the capital of the western Indian state of Maharashtra.

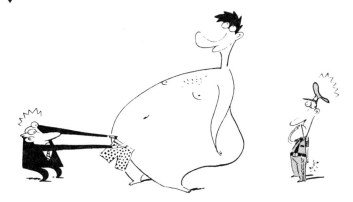

The higher court acquitted him after he proved that the underwear summoned in evidence was undersized, the news agency said.

Kerala High Court Justice K. Padmanabhan, who heard Salvador's plea, asked him to wear the underwear in the presence of a court official.

The official submitted to the judge that the underwear was too small for the accused and that despite all his efforts to wriggle into it, he "miserably failed."

In his defense before the lower court the year before, Salvador had maintained that the underwear produced by the prosecution was not his, because he hadn't worn underwear ever since arriving in the warm coastal state. But the lower court had rejected Salvador's argument and sent him to prison.

"Soft" Judge Sets Stiff Bail

BIRMINGHAM, ALA. (AP) — After being needled by the mayor for being too soft on criminals, a judge raised a theft suspect's bond from $5,000 to $9 trillion.

District Judge Jack Montgomery declined to explain how he arrived at $9 trillion, nearly three times the national debt of $3.2 trillion.

The judge raised the bond after initially setting it at $5,000, said a deputy at Jefferson County Jail, where the suspect remained.

Montgomery said no one had contacted him about reconsidering bond for Isaac Peterson, thirty-four, who was arrested on a theft charge.

"This is so he doesn't get in any more trouble," the judge said. "I could have set his bond at nothing, or I could have let him out on his signature."

At a city council meeting, Mayor Richard Arrington said the judge repeatedly enabled suspects with serious criminal backgrounds to be released by setting low bonds.

Arrington cited Peterson, who he said has recently been arrested eight times on charges of burglary and receiving stolen property. Each time, bond ranged from $500 to $5,000. For someone with Peterson's criminal history it should be higher, the mayor said.

Montgomery said he has set high bonds before, including a $2.6 billion bond in one case he could not recall. "I have a big mouth and people are always taking potshots at me," Montgomery said. "I have gone so far out on a limb that I've built a nest out there."

Foul-mouthed Parrot Returned to Owner

Spokane, Wash. (AP) — When the green parrot beneath the blue blanket told police officers what they could do with themselves, they knew they'd found Buddy.

The foul-mouthed fowl, pilfered from its perch in an art-store window during a break-in, was returned Thursday to owner Claudia Myers.

A tip led police to the apartment to which Buddy had been taken.

A warrant told police to be on the lookout for a

parrot that dismisses people with an unprintable suggestion. When police lifted the blanket over its cage, the parrot gave them the surly greeting and they knew it was Buddy.

Buddy, the mascot of Spokane Art Supplies for twenty years, seemed happy to be reunited with Myers, Sgt. Earl Ennis said.

"It just started squawking and squawking," Ennis said. "You could tell it missed her."

Buddy suffered a sprained wing but was otherwise in good shape. He apparently didn't pick up any more bad language from his captors, Myers said—at thirty-five he's a bit old to learn new tricks.

Cops Clueless to Catch Callous Cat Killer

SEATTLE, WASH. (Reuters) — Seattle police are hunting a ruthless serial killer—of cats.

The gunman, who picks off his feline victims from a car as they sit peering out of windows, has killed six cats outright and wounded two others so badly they had to be destroyed.

He even mistakenly shot a stuffed animal, knocking it across a living room.

Detectives say they want to catch the gunman, who operates in suburbs south of Seattle, before he injures or kills someone. But so far they have turned up no suspects, and the only clues they have are a few .22 caliber slugs or shell casings.

If caught, the suspect will face charges of reckless endangerment, which could lead to several years in jail as well as a welter of lawsuits from grieving cat owners.

India's Longest Criminal Trial Ends After Thirty-three Years

NEW DELHI (AP) — A court acquitted four men of fraud after a thirty-three-year trial that cost the state more than 130 times the amount the men were accused of appropriating, newspapers reported.

"This trial is the biggest waste of public time and money," Judge V. B. Gupta was quoted as saying in *The Hindu* daily.

News reports said the case was the longest criminal trial ever recorded in India.

The newspaper quoted Judge Gupta as saying that the prosecution had failed to prove the fraud charges, despite the thirty-three years of hearings. He said that over the years the cost of the trial mounted to a total of $588,235.

As the trial dragged on, only twelve of the sixty-four witnesses cited by the prosecution ever testified, and sixteen others died, the newspaper said.

India's judicial system is well known for its slowness.

Thieves Steal Guinness Book of Records *Rice Grains From Indian*

NEW DELHI (AFP) — An Indian painter claimed that thieves stole six grains from his collection of rice on which he had inscribed portraits to earn an entry last year into the *Guinness Book of Records*, police here said.

Painter Dipak Sayal said thieves made away with his briefcase containing the rice, on which he had painted portraits of Indian statesmen. The collection was recently put on display in a tourism carnival near New Delhi.

However, Mr. Sayal told the police that the thieves had missed his best piece of work, a single grain on which he had painted 813 characters.

Mr. Sayal's briefcase was taken from his parked car in the city, police said, adding that a search was on for the thieves as well as the six grains of rice.

Mr. Sayal, a college student from northern Haryana state, has painted portraits of world leaders on rice and vertically balanced coins, and drawn the world map on eggshells without missing any detail.

His latest project has been to copy holy Hindu scripts on a single strand of hair.

Can I Serve You, Officer?

PHOENIX (AP) — A fast-food chain's problem here is nothing to sneeze at.

A Jack in the Box cook has been arrested for allegedly blowing his nose onto a hamburger he served a policeman.

The company canceled its commercials for two weeks because so many radio stations were making gags about the incident.